CW00854672

The Guardian of the Threshold

The Souls Awaken

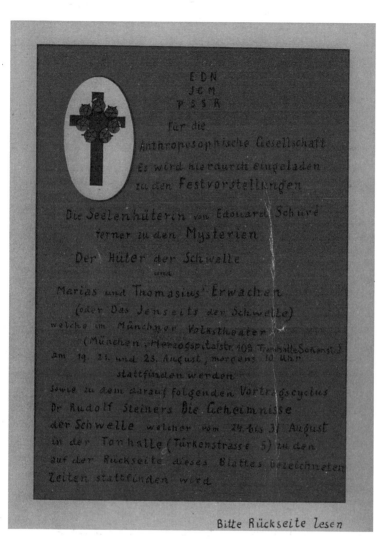

The original 1913 announcement for the first performances of the 4th Mystery Drama, where it is given the title:
Maria's and Johannes' Awakening
(or *The Other Side of the Threshold*)

Rudolf Steiner's
Third and Fourth Mystery Dramas

The Guardian of the Threshold

The Souls Awaken

Translated by Richard Ramsbotham

Wynstones
Press

Published by

Wynstones Press
Stourbridge
England.

www.wynstonespress.com

First edition 2016

Printed in UK.

ISBN 9780 946206 797

Contents

Introduction

A New Beginning

It may appear strange to find a book containing only the 3rd and 4th parts of a series of 4 plays. There is a distinction, however, between Rudolf Steiner's first two and last two Mystery Dramas that perhaps justifies the 3rd and 4th Mystery Dramas being published on their own. For Rudolf Steiner only described these last two Mystery Dramas as having been written by him ("von Rudolf Steiner.") The first two he described as having been written through him ("durch Rudolf Steiner.") The first two Mystery Dramas have the character therefore of having somehow been 'given' – whereas the last two are more to be seen as having been individually won.

Rudolf Steiner's first Mystery Drama, as is well-known, has a close kinship with Goethe's 'Fairy Tale' – *The Green Snake and the Beautiful Lily*. In Steiner's first draft of the 1st Mystery Drama the names of the characters are the same as those in Goethe's Fairy Tale. Only in his second draft did Steiner give the characters new names – for example, *Lily* became Maria; *Man (Prince)* became Johannes Thomasius; *Snake* became the Other Maria; *1st Will-o'-the-Wisp* became Capesius; *2nd Will-o'-the-Wisp* became Strader.

After the uplifting and transformative ending of the 1st Mystery Drama, however, the 2nd Mystery Drama ends far more problematically – with Johannes held 'captive' by Lucifer, Capesius overwhelmed by his inner experiences, Strader in a state of spiritual sleep, etc. In the third Mystery Drama a new impulse is therefore necessary if the characters are finally to win through, in a way befitting the present, to what *The Green Snake and the Beautiful Lily* depicted in fairy tale form.

Goethe's tale ends with: a new temple having raised itself into the light of day; the river between the sense-world and the spiritual world having been bridged; and many people now crossing this bridge in both directions. Steiner's last two Mystery Dramas depict, not in fairy tale images, but in dramatic scenes: the opening up of the Mysteries to mankind; the characters' individual and inter-connected struggles to bridge, consciously, the sense and spirit-worlds; and, made possible by these spiritual developments, the search for new forms of cultural, social and economic life, appropriate for the present day.

The Third Mystery Drama begins almost immediately after the decision has been taken to open up the Mysteries. Although the 3rd and 4th plays build, of course, on what has preceded them in the first two plays, they must also be seen, therefore, as representing a new beginning.

The Guardian of the Threshold and the Temple

The third Mystery Drama comes to a spiritual culmination in its final scene, where the traditional Temple of the "Mystic Brotherhood" is renewed and transformed through the work of Benedictus and his pupils.* This transformation involves Johannes, Capesius and Strader becoming able, not through tradition, but through their own individual accomplishment, to represent the three different attributes of Wisdom, Beauty ('Schein') and Strength. In order to achieve this, they are each brought, in widely differing ways, into the realm of the Guardian of the Threshold. In a lecture of 8 December 1918 (GA 186) Rudolf Steiner describes three different ways of encountering the Guardian of the Threshold, connected to the attributes of *Wisdom, Beauty* and *Strength*, which closely parallel what Johannes, Capesius and Strader undergo. Steiner further describes these three different experiences as relating to what occurs when a person of *Eastern Europe, Central Europe* or *Western Europe*, respectively, encounters the Guardian of the Threshold.

Once Johannes, Capesius and Strader have passed through these trials, individually, they are encouraged by Benedictus to unite their work with that of both the others, and thus to "form a trinity" which could "do much to bring about a healing/ Of mankind." (Scene IX) Among the many profound ways one may think about this, it certainly also points towards a harmonious collaboration between West, Middle and East. Maria is then able to let a new *fourth* quality – namely, spiritual love – stream into the Temple.

In what might be seen as a prophetic picture, the end of the 3rd Mystery Drama thus depicts the potential transformation of world culture, in all spheres of life, in accordance with the true possibilities and needs of today.

---

* In Benedictus, as the character-notes to the 4th Mystery Drama describe: "that spiritual stream comes to expression... which wishes to put a living and present spiritual life in the place of a merely traditional one".

The Souls Awaken and the Factory

Not a single scene of the 4th Mystery Drama takes place within the 'Temple'. What was achieved at the end of the 3rd Mystery Drama receives, in fact, hardly any mention. As we see from the very first scene of the play, the action has stepped out of the Temple and into the everyday reality of a modern factory. The question has become, therefore, whether our contemporary civilization itself is now able to be transformed.

The action of the 4th Mystery Drama is initiated by the "project" Hilary has conceived of and has begun to try and realize. Hilary is the owner of a factory or sawmill (ein Sägewerk) which he inherited from his father and which has, until now, has been run in well-tried, efficient, traditional ways. His "project" consists of Benedictus and his pupils – Johannes, Maria, Capesius and Strader – helping to renew and transform all aspects of the factory's life, and thus bringing their transformative potential right 'down' into the realms of social, economic and even technological life.

There are also many other aspects to *The Souls Awaken*, which is not only longer than the other Mystery Dramas, but is also unprecedented in the range of spiritual experience it explores. The "project" that Hilary hopes and attempts to realize remains, however, an essential concern, affecting all the characters, from the beginning of the play to the end.

The First World War

The 4th Mystery Drama was written and first performed in 1913. A 5th Mystery Drama was intended to have been performed in August 1914. The outbreak of the First World War not only made this impossible, but also gave a tragic negative answer to the question of whether the spiritual, social and economic life of Europe could be transformed in the light of the true needs and possibilities of our time. Far from there being a positive transformation of world culture, recognizing the different tasks of West, Middle and East, the powers of the West forcefully imposed their dominance on the world, and have continued to do so until today.

This danger is also visible in the 4th Mystery Drama, where the firm's Manager, influenced by the "Western" Brother, Romanus, prevents Hilary's project going further, by only being prepared to work with Strader, among Benedictus's pupils, regardless of the fact that Strader sees no purpose in his work if it cannot be carried out in harmonious cooperation with that of the others.

There are other factors as well, which conspire to prevent Hilary's project succeeding. But insofar as the factory is in some way representative of contemporary civilization, it is certainly symptomatic that the individuals linked to the West fail to question their one-sided dominance, until tragedy occurs.

Dating Riddle

The 3rd Mystery Drama was written in 1912 and the 4th Mystery Drama in 1913. The events of the 3rd Mystery Drama, however, are described as occurring "13 years" after those of the 1st Mystery Drama. As the 1st Mystery Drama was written in 1910, one might therefore see the events of the 3rd Mystery Drama as taking place in 1923 – a year of huge importance for the anthroposophical movement. The events of the 4th Mystery Drama are described as taking place "one year" after those of the 3rd Mystery Drama – and might also therefore be related to 1924.

"All That is Needed"

At the end of the last of the series of lectures given to accompany the first performances of the 3rd Mystery Drama, Rudolf Steiner commented, somewhat strangely, on the possibility of his no longer being alive, and said:

"If from this moment I could no longer either speak or write, were people only to build further on what they already have – I no longer being present – if people looked for the meaning in all they have been given, they would find all that is needed." (31 August 1912)

As the lectures he had been giving had to do with the 3rd Mystery Drama, one might ask whether the 3rd Mystery Drama does not itself somehow contain "all that is needed", albeit as seed-potential, expressed in artistic form.

1923 and *The Guardian of the Threshold*

The European-wide tragedy of the First World War (1914-1918), followed by the tragedy to Rudolf Steiner's life's work, and to the anthroposophical movement, of the burning of the First Goetheanum (31 December 1922), meant that by 1923 there must have seemed little possibility for those connected to Rudolf Steiner's work to "build further on what they already have". Like the charred rubble of the First Goetheanum, the anthroposophical movement seemed in many ways to be in ruins. In the face of this tragedy, the 1923 "Christmas Conference" opened the spiritual doorways once again to a vast inflowing of resurrective and redemptive forces. The far-reaching transformation and renewal of the "Temple" at the end of the 3rd Mystery Drama can be seen, I think, to stand in a mysterious inner relationship to what would later take place at Christmas 1923.

1924 and *The Souls Awaken*

The events of the 4th Mystery Drama may likewise be seen to stand in a relationship to much that took place in 1924. Rudolf Steiner concerned himself in 1924, as never before, with the unfolding of the life between death and rebirth in connection with the detailed realities of karma and reincarnation. Scenes V and VI (in the spiritual worlds before the characters' present lives) and scenes VII and VIII (in Ancient Egypt) explore these realities on an unprecedented scale within the Mystery Dramas.

Moreover, after the infinite spiritual potential of Christmas 1923, 1924 demanded of the anthroposophical movement and society that it realize its intentions on earth – just as the characters in the 4th Mystery Drama leave the Temple behind and engage with contemporary civilization, setting about the task of transforming Hilary's factory.

Hilary's "project" founders under the intensity of the demands it places on people, as well as through the unseen spiritual opposition launched against it. This may also be seen to relate to what occurred in the anthroposophical movement in 1924, when tragic differences between members began to develop, powerful spiritual opposition was also at work, and Rudolf Steiner, by the end of the year, had become too ill to lecture and died in early 1925.

Beyond Tragedy

The 4th Mystery Drama, however, goes infinitely farther than mere tragedy. It passes, one could say, unflinchingly *through* tragedy to new paths and possibilities for the future. By the end of the play, the main characters – Johannes, Maria, Strader and Capesius – have all overcome the trials and obstacles that had previously prevented their full participation in Hilary's project. Even Hilary's Manager, who had directly opposed the project, eventually undergoes an inner change.

By the end of the play, therefore, nothing essential stands in the way any longer of a whole new beginning being made, should the right moment for this appear. A prerequisite, however, for this to be able to take place, is described by Benedictus in his final speech, where he states that his pupils, from now on, must clearly perceive the workings of Ahriman through all his ever-changing disguises. If they can do this, they will still be able to achieve their goals in future: "*Even then/When over bright and fully-wakened spirit vision,/Grey, bleak Ahriman (…) Attempts to spread the darkening night of chaos.*"

About the Translations

Rudolf Steiner wrote his four Mystery Dramas almost exclusively in blank verse (iambic pentameter). The following translation of *The Guardian of the Threshold* is also in iambic pentameter, and where Steiner makes use of a different rhythm, as in the speeches of the Soul Forces, I have also adhered to this, with only a few very slight variations. (Occasionally, a letter in brackets indicates that a syllable should ber omitted, when speaking. E.g. "mechanic(a)lly" – page 94). These strict formal demands seemed appropriate, given the strict demands faced by the characters in their encounters with the Guardian of the Threshold.

The translation of the *The Souls Awaken* is in free verse. (It has, in other words, no strict metre.) The comparative freedom of this, with the possibility of much shorter lines, also appeared appropriate for the frequently very contemporary character of this play. The underlying rhythm of the whole, however, is still predominantly iambic.

Both translations were written for particular productions of the plays. They are both completely new translations from the original German. Regarding their form, however, I was influenced by – and acknowledge my indebtedness to – Alexander Gifford's blank verse translation of the 3rd Mystery Drama; and Michael Burton's and Adrian Locher's free verse translation of the 4th Mystery Drama.

In the first announcements of the 4th Mystery Drama Rudolf Steiner named it: *"Maria's and Johannes' Awakening* (or *The Other Side of the Threshold)"* [*"Marias und Thomasius' Erwachen* (oder *Das Jenseits der Schwelle)"*]. In the play-text itself, however, Steiner gave it the title: *The Souls' Awakening* [*Der Seelen Erwachen*]. When one hears this title, in English, it is unclear if the word "Souls" is singular or plural. I have therefore chosen to translate the title as: *The Souls Awaken.*

Richard Ramsbotham
June 2016.

Rudolf Steiner's Third Mystery Drama

The Guardian of the Threshold

Characters, Figures and Events

The Guardian of the Threshold depicts, in a series of dramatic scenes, events in the soul-lives and spiritual lives of the characters. These scenes continue the events in my earlier dramatic representations of life – *The Portal of Initiation* and *The Trial of the Soul* (Rudolf Steiner's first and second Mystery Dramas – tr.). Together with this one, the three plays form a whole.

In *The Guardian of the Threshold* the following characters and beings appear:

I.   **The Bearers of the Spiritual Element:**
1.   **Benedictus,** the leader of the Temple of the Sun and the teacher of a number of people who appear in *The Guardian of the Threshold.* (The Temple of the Sun is only referred to in the *The Portal of Initiation* and *The Trial of the Soul.*)
2.   **Hilarius Gottgetreu** – Hilary – Grand Master of a Mystic Association (or Brotherhood). (In *The Trial of the Soul* he was shown in a former incarnation as the Grand Master of a spiritual Brotherhood.)
3.   **Johannes Thomasius,** a pupil of Benedictus.

II.   **The Bearers of the Element of Devotion:**
4.   **Magnus Bellicosus,** named Germanus (in *The Portal of Initiation*), the Preceptor of the Mystic Association (Brotherhood).
5.   **Albert Torquatus,** named Theodosius in *The Portal of Initiation,* the Master of Ceremonies of the Mystic Association (Brotherhood).
6.   **Professor Capesius.**

III.   **The Bearers of the Element of Will:**
7.   **Friedrich Trautmann,** named 'Romanus' in *The Portal of Initiation,* Master of Ceremonies in the Mystic Association (or Brotherhood). The reincarnation of the second Master of Ceremonies of the spiritual Brotherhood in *The Trial of the Soul.*
8.   **Theodora,** a seeress. (With her the element of Will has been transformed into natural seership.)
9.   **Dr Strader.**

IV.   **The Bearers of the Element of Soul:**
        10. Maria, a pupil of Benedictus.
        11. Felix Balde.
        12. Felicia Balde, his wife.

V.   **Beings from the Spiritual World:**
        Lucifer.
        Ahriman.

VI.   **Beings of the Human Spiritual Element:**
        The Double of Johannes.
        The Soul of Theodora.
        The Guardian of the Threshold.
        Philia, Astrid and **Luna** – the spiritual beings who mediate the connection of the human soul-forces with the universe.
        The Other Philia, the spiritual being who hinders the connection of the soul-forces with the universe.
        The Voice of Conscience.

These spiritual beings are not intended allegorically or symbolically, but as realities, which are equally present for spiritual knowledge as are physical personalities.

1.   **Ferdinand Reinecke** (fox).
2.   **Michael Edelmann** (nobleman).
3.   **Bernard Redlich** (honest).
4.   **Francesca Demut** (humble).
5.   **Mary Treufels** (faithful as a rock).
6.   **Louisa Fürchegott** (god-fearing).
7.   **Friedrich Geist** (spirit).
8.   **Caspar Stürmer** (stormer).
9.   **Georg Wahrmund** (truemouth).
10.   **Maria Kühne** (bold).
11.   **Hermine Hauser** (homely).
12.   **Katharina Ratsam** (good advice).

These are the reincarnations of the twelve peasant men and women in *The Trial of the Soul.*

The events of *The Guardian of the Threshold* take place about thirteen years after those of *The Portal of Initiation*. The way in which lives are repeated in *The Guardian of the Threshold* should not be taken as a generally valid rule, but rather as something that can take place at a turning point of time. The events of scene eight, for example, between Strader and the twelve citizens are thus only possible at such a period of time. The spiritual beings appearing in *The Guardian of the Threshold* are in no way to be thought of as allegorical or symbolical; those who know a spiritual world to be a reality, may very well present beings such as these, which have just as much reality there as beings have in the sense-world. Anyone who takes these beings to be allegories or symbols misunderstands the entire character of the events in *The Guardian of the Threshold*. That spiritual beings do not have a human form, as they must necessarily do in a dramatic presentation, goes without saying. If the writer of this 'series of soul events in dramatic scenes' had considered these beings to be allegories, he would not have depicted them in the way he does. The division of the characters into groups (3 x 4) was not sought after nor placed, before-hand, as the basis of the play; it resulted – afterwards, for thinking – from the events depicted, which were conceived completely on their own and which create such a division by themselves. It would never have occurred to the author to place them there as a foundation from the beginning. To mention them here, however, as having resulted from it, may be permitted.

Rudolf Steiner

Scene One

A room of which the basic colour is indigo blue. It is intended as the entrance hall leading to the room in which a Mystic Brotherhood carries out its work. Twelve people are present, engaged in informal discussion; they are all interested, in one way or another, in the activities of the Mystic Brotherhood. In addition, Felix Balde and Dr. Strader are present. The scenes of the play depict events which happen about thirteen years after those of 'The Portal of Initiation'.

Ferdinand Reinecke

    So here we are. Each one of us has come
    In answer to the strangest invitation
    Sent out to us by those who've always kept
    Apart from folk like us, believing in
    Their very, very special spirit-goals.
    Yet now, apparently, the cosmic plan
    Has been unveiled before their spirit-eyes
    That they are meant to link themselves with folk
    Who face life's struggles on their own, without
    Initiation in their temple's rites.
    Personally, I've never had much time
    For spiritual groups that have to work in secret.
    I'd rather stay with healthy human thinking
    And common sense. And listen, friends – I'll bet
    This spirit-brotherhood that's called us here
    Has absolutely no intention to
    Enlighten us about their highest goals.
    With nebulous dark mystic formulas
    They'll keep us in the temple's outer rooms –
    And use us to gain popular support
    For what they want to do. Thus they intend
    To make us blind and passive helpers while
    They arrogantly lord it over us –
    Our spiritual superiors. They will
    Not think us capable of taking one

Small step towards the real light-
Filled treasures that their sanctuary conceals.
I'll tell you what their real being is:
Vast spiritual pride and trickery, dressed up
To seem quite humble in their prophets' robes.
We should leave now and not have anything
To do with all the "wisdom" they proclaim.
But so it does not seem we're just rejecting
Out of hand their holy work without
Considering it – I would advise you all
At least to hear whatever they may say –
What they intend, these "wisdom-bringers" – then
Just follow what your common sense dictates.
If you make this into your guide and leader,
You'll never fall for all the traps and lures
Laid out for you by these great mystagogues.

Michael Edelmann

I do not know, I cannot even guess
What spirit-treasures are entrusted to
These people, who desire to find a bridge
To us. But I know several people who
Are members of this group and find each one
Of them a fine, upstanding person. Yes –
They never say a word about the source
From where their knowledge springs; they keep this secret.
Their deeds, though, and the way they live their lives
Reveal the goodness of the source from which
They draw. And all that springs from their circle
Bears unmistakably the mark of true
And loving kindness. Therefore I am sure
The reason will be good that leads them now
To wish to join with those, like us, for whom
The mystic ways are strange, yet understand
The search for truth and for life's highest goals.

Bernard Redlich:

> You go too far. I think we should be cautious.
> The mystics clearly feel their time is over
> Or will be soon. For do you think, in future,
> That any rational mind will care that much
> What "mystic temples" preach about the truth?
> So when we hear what aims these "brothers" have,
> If they sound sensible to common minds,
> It would be reasonable to join with them.
> But then – if they desire to cross the bridge
> That separates their lofty light-filled world
> From this one – then there's no more mystic robes
> And special airs and privilege. They'll have
> No greater nor no lesser value than
> The way they're valued in the popular mind.

Franziska Demut

> Oh dear. What nonsenses we hear. You seem
> Completely blind to that true spirit-light
> That's always shone its rays of wisdom through
> The world, from mystery centres such as this one,
> Illumining and comforting and healing souls.
> But only those who let this light invade
> Their heart, and feel it fill their souls with warmth,
> Will recognize the value of this hour.
> It is the moment when – even for those
> Who feel themselves too weak to undergo
> Stern trials of soul in hidden sanctuaries –
> The Mysteries are opening their doors.

Maria Treufels

> You're right that many signs make clear today
> That much will have to be transformed in souls
> Who seek the spirit-guidance of mankind.
> However, very little indicates
> That mysticism and the mystic paths

Can give to human souls the strength they need.
Our times, it seems to me, need leaders who,
When they employ their natural gifts unite
True genius with skill, and so can feel
Within their work on earth the purpose of
Their lives. Such people even seek the roots
Of spiritual deeds within the mother-ground
Of true reality, and thus, without
Illusions, walk in ways of service for
The world. I'm utterly convinced of this.
It's Dr. Strader, therefore, in my eyes,
Who has what's needed, more than all these mystics,
To point the new way forward for mankind.
How long have we all felt so painfully
That through the wonderful creations of
Technology, the soul is shackled, bound,
That by itself would freely seek the spirit.
But suddenly there is a hope at last
That noone would have dreamed about before.
In Strader's workshop wonderous machines
Are working now, in miniature, which soon,
When working on a larger scale, will quite
Transform the nature of technology –
And take away from it that sting, that weight,
That so oppresses many souls today.

Strader   I thank you for these words so full of hope
About my work. It does indeed seem that
It has succeeded. Even though there's still
A certain bridge to cross between our trials
And our experiments – and application.
But technically, so far as we can see,
It's all completely feasible. I do
Not wish to seem immodest, but perhaps
I may say more about this and describe

The feelings that have fired me in my work.
My starting-point was this – that looking back
At human history we plainly see:
The more the human spirit's learned to master
The forces that control the physical world,
The more has human labour grown divorced
From heart-filled feeling and become a thing
Quite void of soul. Our work grows ever more
Mechanical and governed by technology
And so does life itself. You can't
Imagine how much thought has been put in
To solve this question. How to stop machines
From laming us within our souls and spirits?
It led to very little, asking just
How people should relate. I too have spent
Long hours wracked in thought upon this question,
But all my efforts always led me nowhere.
I nearly reached the bitter point of view
That it is written in world destiny
That all our triumphs in the realm of matter
Must stand opposed to progress in the spirit.
But then, amazingly, as if by "chance",
Engaged in work completely unrelated,
The thoughts poured out of me that showed the way
At last to solve this question. After that
Each day brought new experiments until
We witnessed, unmistakably, this great
Harmonic resonance of forces, which,
Just purely technically, will bring the freedom
Necessary to evolve in spirit.
Once developed fully, never more
Will people have to live demeaning lives
In mechanized environments that sap
All dignity and real human life.
The forces of technology will so

Be shared among mankind that everything
A person needs to carry out their work
May comfortably be theirs to use, in their
Own homes, and fashioned just as they determine.
I've needed, first, to tell you of these hopes,
To show the background for my views about
The invitation you have all received
To meet the Rosicrucian brotherhood.
When souls begin at last to find themselves
And to unfold their full potential, then
May impulses be blessed and come to good
That link us with realities of spirit.
If you would see this rightly, understand
The open gesture of the Rosicrucians
Is wholly in accord with many other
Signs we see. The spirit-brothers wish
To freely share their gifts with all, because
These are what everyone, in truth, requires.

Felix Balde   These words we've heard are spoken by a man
Who has enriched our time with mighty gifts
Within the world of sense. Within this realm
There is noone to rival Dr. Strader.
Myself, by travelling very different paths,
I've also found the true needs of the soul.
Perhaps, therefore, I too may be allowed
To speak. When I was young I always felt
That destiny itself was guiding me
To seek those treasures hidden deep within
Our being's inmost core. I felt that there
Was to be found the light of wisdom that
Could then illumine all our earthly goals.
By grace I learned to walk the mystic's path,
In solitude and quiet contemplation.
Upon such paths I saw how everything

That makes man master of the realm of matter
Just leaves him blind and stumbling through darkness.
And all the knowledge gained by sense and reason
Is also but a guessing in the dark.
The way to reach the true and living light
Is only by the mystic paths. Not everyone
Can find these, though, as I did, without help.
Our scientific knowledge must remain
A soulless corpse as long as it rejects
The light that, since the genesis of earth,
Has shone within the truest Mysteries.
So if this Temple – on whose threshold light-
Filled roses wrap themselves in glory round
The sign of death – extends to you its hand:
Receive that hand with love into your own.

Luise Fürchtegott

Well thank you, sir. But if we have a sense
For our own dignity, we must rely
Upon our individual power of judgement
In seeking for the spirit and ourselves.
Don't blindly trust the leadership of others;
In doing so you'll lose your very self.
Even the light that shines as wisdom, deep
Within our inmost core, we'd like to feel –
Does not deserve our spirit's recognition
Unless it's possible to prove its truth.
For light can all too well be dangerous
If on no evidence we follow it.
For all too often what a person thinks
To be a vision of the grounds of worlds
Is nothing but the soul's projected wish.

Friedrich Geist

We all should feel the need to understand
The mystics' spirit-path. It seems to me

We'll only find illusion not the truth,
If taking not one step upon their path
We think to know just what their vision is.
The mystic, though, they say, relates to truth
Like someone who will climb a mountain peak
Because they wish to see the heavenly view.
They wait till they have reached the top and do
Not try and tell themselves beforehand what
That vision is, to which their journey leads.

Ferdinand Reinecke

It's utterly irrelevant right now
To ask how people should relate to truth.
I can assure you that this brotherhood
Has no desire to hear our views on this.
A quite particular event, you see,
So I have heard, has forced the brothers to
Invite us here. And the event is this:
Johannes, who I think you know
Was once a member of some spiritual group
With "mystic goals". And he has now disguised,
In forms of knowledge everyone can trust,
The wisdom that "initiation" brings.
Through this he's now a most successful author –
Who's loudly praised amidst the widest circles,
For writings which, beneath their cloak of logic,
Contain just wild, fanatic, mystic ramblings.
Now even many serious researchers
Extol the gospel that Johannes brings –
And thus his fame is spreading dangerously.
So what do the initiates make of that?
They're terrified. If this goes on, the view
That all the secrets of initiation
Are theirs alone would be ridiculous.
They therefore try and take under their own

Protection all that's happening through Johannes.
They want to make it seem they've always known
This gospel would be given to the world
To serve their work – that all of this was planned!
I tell you all – if at this gathering now,
When soon the brothers shall appear, they are
Successful in persuading us to join
Their cause – then they will publish to the world
That everything Johannes writes and says
Was given out by powers of destiny –
And thus, they hope, even just common sense
Will understand, or better still believe,
The world-importance of their brotherhood.

Caspar Stürmer
He's absolutely right. It really is
Incredible this "mystic school" can claim
It somehow guides mankind. This only shows
How little they esteem the progress made
By healthy powers of judgement since it has
Been proved that nature and the soul can be
Explained in purely mechanistic terms.
To independent minds it's very sad,
To say the least, to see a mind as clear
As Dr. Strader's fall for this delusion.
Someone who's mastered mechanistic forces,
Like him, should know that true psychology
Must firmly do away with mysticism.
The pseudo-science put out by Johannes
Should warn a man like Strader that even
The sharpest minds, if they make this mistake,
Will soon be chasing wildest fantasies.
Johannes, if he'd disciplined himself
For his creative work, by thinking that's
In tune with nature, with his gifts could well

Have come to real fruits of knowledge. But
Instead he sought the mystic ways of art,
A route to catastrophic error. Well,
This spirit-brotherhood knew instantly
How they could make this error serve their goals.
They hope they'll gain great praise and recognition –
And will do if you all are gullible –
For it will seem Johannes now has proved
Their mystic knowledge, which is but a dream.

Georg Wahrmund

That anyone can utter words like these,
So painful for the listener, clearly shows
How still today the insight we can gain
When we behold the course of spiritual life
Has barely yet begun to be evolved.
Look back into the very earliest days
Before that science, which has its heyday now,
Was even present as a seed, and try
And understand what lived in human souls.
It will be plain for you that in this hour
This brotherhood will carry out a deed
The wise plans of the world have long foreseen.
This moment has been waiting. It could not
Occur till that great work had been accomplished
Johannes finally achieved. Completely new
Will be the way the spirit-light may shine
In him – illumining the human soul.
This light already shone in everything
That people have created on the earth.
But where did this light have its source? This light
That shone in human souls unconsciously?
The signs all point towards that mystic wisdom
That had its home within the Mysteries
Before mankind was guided by its reason.

The spirit-brotherhood that's called us here
Wishes to let that Mystic Light now shine
Upon the work that bravely seeks to climb
From human thinking to true spirit-knowledge.
And we, who by some grace have been allowed
Within this sacred place at this great hour
Shall be the first, as non-initiates,
To see the spark of heavenly light leap forth
From heights of spirit to the depths of soul.

Marie Kühne

Johannes has no need of the support
Or blessing given by the Rosicrucians.
For in a serious, scientific way
He has described the journey of the soul
Through many lives and through spirit-realms.
And through this deed that lofty, radiant light
To which the Mystic Temples claim to lead
Now stands revealed even to people who
Have never yet approached such temples' thresholds.
Johannes well deserves the recognition
That he's received in such abundance, for
He's found the way to give to thinking freedom,
Which Mystery Schools have long sought to deny.

Hermine Hauser

And so the Rosicrucians in the future
Will only live in people's memories.
The very thing that they're announcing now,
When it becomes aware of its own power,
Will undermine the ground the Temple stands on.
They boldly seek to join in future what
Lives in the Mysteries with science and reason.
What could be more ironic? He to whom
They now open their doors so willingly –
Johannes – in the future will be seen
As he brought about the Temple's doom.

Strader   I was severely criticized for saying
That if we see things rightly we will wish
To help, together with this Brotherhood,
Take further what Johannes has achieved.
One stormy gentleman found this view "sad
To say the least" – for surely I should know,
He said, the dangers of such mysticism
To any genuine knowledge and research.
The strange thing is, though, that I always felt
I understand the best that spiritual life
When utterly absorbed and focussed on the power
Connecting me with mechanisms of
My own creation. Thus the way that I
Related to my work and my inventions
Revealed to me what lives in Mystery Centres.
I'd often think while I was working: what,
I wonder, would I be to someone, if
They only tried to know about me how
Those forces work I placed in these machines?
And what, by contrast, am I to a soul
To whom I lovingly am able to reveal
My inmost self? I'm very grateful to
Such thoughts, which opened up the door to that
What truly lives within the Mystics' teachings.
Through this I know, though uninitiated,
That in the Mysteries the souls of gods
May lovingly encounter human souls.

Katharina Ratsam
The words that Dr. Strader has just spoken
Of the life within the Mysteries
Resound, I hope, even to those of us
Who have not neared before the temple-thresholds
That only an initiate can cross,
But are not wholly strangers to their teachings.

It isn't hard to see why, in the past,
Our ancestors perceived the Mystics as
The enemies of true belief and light.
They had no chance to even intimate
What could be hidden so mysteriously
Within the Temple walls. But things have changed.
No longer do the Mystics hide their light.
They share quite openly what can be known
To non-initiates. And many souls
Who have received this light and felt it quicken
Have felt, through this, the forces of their souls,
That had been slumbering unconsciously,
Now suddenly awake to life within them.

Three knocks are heard.

Felix Balde   They're here! The spirit-masters of this place.
Or will be very soon. Then all of us
May hear the words they say. But only those
Who are entirely free from prejudice
Will understand them truly and recognize
Their light. The living power of the initiates
Will show its strength to hearts and wills that are
Prepared to sacrifice illusion
When they can sense the shining light of truth.
This power, though, is quite without effect
When wills are firmly set in their illusion
And have already slain the sense for truth.

Ferdinand Reinecke

Such words are valid, when a person wants
Through self-reflection on what lives within
Their inner world to get to know themselves.
However, when this Mystic Group appears
It would be better to remember the
Reliable reports that history

Has handed down about such "brotherhoods".
They show that many people let themselves
Be lured into the "Mystic Temples" when
They learned, through occult-sounding words, that they
Would rise within these temples, step by step,
From lower grades of wisdom to the higher,
And reach at last the vision of the spirit.
What happened to such people? Well, they tell
That first they had to look at certain signs
And symbols and to think about their meaning.
They hoped that later, in the higher grades,
The hidden wisdom in these signs would be
Unveiled to them. But when they got there, what
They found was that the "spiritual Masters" knew,
In fact, very little about these signs,
And offered only trivialities
About the meaning of the world and life.
And those who weren't befuddled by these words,
Or duped, or captured by their vanity,
Could see right through it – and would walk away.
It might be good, therefore, I think, right now,
If we're prepared to hear not only fine
And elevating words, but also, maybe,
One or two historical reports.

Again, three knocks are heard.

The Grand Master of the Mystic Brotherhood, Hilarius Gottgetreu, enters. Behind him follow Magnus Bellicosus, the second Preceptor; Albert Torquatus, the first Master of Ceremonies; and Friedrich Trautmann, the second Master of Ceremonies. The people already gathered divide and group themselves on either side of the room.

Friedrich Trautmann

Dear friends, you all are very welcome here.
This is a precious moment, both for you
And for ourselves – and bridges a divide
That has not ever yet been crossed. You stand
Before our Temple's ancient sacred portal
And will, we hope, from now on join your ways with ours.
No casual whim has called you. *Signs* that our
Highest masters could behold within
The wisely guided scheme of earthly life
Demanded that this call should be sent out.
It has been known that in our times the wise
And holy service of the Mysteries
Should join with general human understanding.
But what the signs revealed to us was this:
Before this could occur, someone must
Appear who would transform the knowledge based
On reason and the senses, so that it
Could truly apprehend the spirit-worlds.
This has happened! Johannes has been able
To give the science of our day a work,
That offers proofs, in its own language, for
Realities of spirit which, before,
Could not be found, except on Mystic Paths
And in the temples of initiation.
This work must now become the solid band
Uniting you with us in spirit-life.
You will be able to experience,
Through this work, the strong foundations of
Our teachings. Through this you'll acquire the strength
To then receive, with confidence, the knowledge
One can only gain on mystic paths.
A life, dear friends, could beautifully unfold,
That brings together general understanding
With all that lies within the Mysteries.

Magnus Bellicosus

> Our brother has described how hidden signs
> Revealed to us the need to call you here
> Before this threshold. Our Master will enlarge
> More deeply on the meaning of this call.
> The task that falls to me is now to tell
> You more of that great man whose work has made
> This moment possible. Johannes was
> A painter, utterly devoted to
> His art, before he felt the spirit-call
> To turn himself to science. As an artist
> He only had developed his unique
> Extraordinary gifts when he had met
> With groups committed to true mysticism.
> They led him to that high Master, who
> Could set him on the path of spirit-vision,
> In accordance with the ways of wisdom.
> And then he painted – borne into the heights
> Of spirit, and experiencing himself
> Amidst the powers of world-creation – paintings
> That could breathe and work like living beings.
> This might have led another artist to strive,
> Remaining in their own particular field,
> For all the highest goals they could attain.
> But for Johannes, this was but the spur
> That urged him on to seek for how to use
> The faculties he had acquired, in such
> A way as best would benefit mankind.
> And it was clear to him, that only then
> Could spiritual knowledge receive a true foundation,
> If science's use of sense and intellect
> Could, with the help of the artistic spirit,
> Be freed from rigid forms, and also strengthened
> Inwardly, and thus experience
> The being of the world. Johannes's

Artistic creativity, that he
Could easily have used to serve himself,
He sacrificed, quite willingly, to serve
The spirit of mankind. Recognize,
Dear friends, the being of this man –
And you will understand the call we sent, and will
No longer hesitate to follow it.

Hilary   In the name of that great Spirit, who
Reveals himself to souls within this sacred
Place, we now appear to all of you,
Who until now were not allowed to hear
The Word that here sounds out its Mysteries.
The powers who guide the hidden goals of Earth
Could not, in primal days of old, reveal
Themselves in light to everyone. For just
As only gradually, with children, must
The forces ripen and grow strong, that later
Lead to knowledge, so did mankind as
A whole need slowly to unfold its powers.
The stirrings of the soul at first were dull,
Which later should prove worthy to behold
The spirit-light that shines in higher worlds.
But at the dawn of life on earth, there were
Sent down, to wisely guide and lead mankind,
Exalted spirit-beings from higher realms.
They brought to birth, within the Mysteries,
The spirit-forces which in secret streamed
Into men's souls, who were quite unaware
Of their exalted leaders. Later, though,
These Masters chose, from out the ranks of men,
Disciples, who through lives of trial and harsh
Renunciation, proved themselves mature
Enough to be initiated in
The sacred teachings of the Mysteries.

And later on, when these disciples of
The first, orig(i)nal Masters showed that they
Were worthy now to guard this sacred treasure,
Their wise, exalted Masters made their way
Back to their true and distant spirit-homes.
Thereafter the disciples of the gods
Themselves selected men who could succeed
Them in their work. And so it carried on
For generations numberless to us.
Even today, all genuine mystic schools
Descend directly from that primal one,
Which stems from higher spirits. We, who serve
Here, humbly carry on that ancient lineage.
We'd never speak of our deserving, just
Of grace bestowed by higher spiritual powers,
Who choose weak men to be their emissaries,
And who entrust to them those sacred treasures,
Which can set free the spirit-light within
The soul. We open up to you, today,
These treasures, friends. The signs are most auspicious;
Within the cosmic plan they now reveal
Themselves, quite clearly, to the spirit-eye.

Ferdinand Reinecke

The reasons that you bring, you say, are found
In far-off cosmic worlds; reasons that
Are meant to prove that we should join with you,
And thus enable the great work of Johannes
To have its full effect for the first time.
However beautiful your words may sound,
They cannot conquer the opinion,
In simple hearts, that if this work indeed
Contains what every human soul requires,
Then it will prove itself by its own power.
Its great significance is said to be

That in it nothing mystical, but science
Itself, supports the truths of spiritual science.
Excuse my asking, but, if this is so,
What can be gained if *praise bestowed upon*
It by the mystics guarantee its full
Success, and not its own inherent worth?

Albert Torquatus

That science that Johannes has, through all
His noble powers of reasoning, unveiled
Before the world, will neither gain nor lose
From our recognition, or from yours.
But through it people then may find the path
On which they can approach true mystic knowledge.
This science will have done but half its work
If it becomes an end and not a path.
It now is up to you to understand
The time has come, the moment has arrived,
For reason and the mystic paths to join.
This deed could quite transform the modern world,
Uplifting it to previously unknown heights,
If carried out at this auspicious hour.

Curtain.

Scene Two

The same room as in the previous scene. Those who had been assembled there originally have left. There are present: Hilarius Gottgetreu, the Grand Master [known as Hilary]; Magnus Bellicosus, the second Preceptor; Albert Torquatus, the first Master of Ceremonies; Friedrich Trautmann, the second Master of Ceremonies; Maria; Johannes Thomasius; of those assembled at the beginning there remain only: Felix Balde, Dr. Strader.

Hilary　　My son, you are most welcome. Now the work
　　　　　You have accomplished must receive the seal
　　　　　Of age old sacred knowledge – and, within
　　　　　This hallowed place, the Rosy Cross bestow
　　　　　Upon it all its sacred power of blessing.
　　　　　What you have brought the world, we now shall offer
　　　　　To the spirit, making it bear fruit,
　　　　　Within those worlds where human power grows ripe,
　　　　　To serve the evolution of the world.

Magnus Bellicosus
　　　　　To give your great work to the world, you've needed
　　　　　Now, for years, to keep apart from much
　　　　　That prior to that was dearest to your soul.
　　　　　You had a spirit-teacher by your side.
　　　　　So that your soul could fully bring to birth
　　　　　In you your individual powers, he left you.
　　　　　You also had a true companion – your
　　　　　Dear friend. She also left you – for you had
　　　　　To find what can be found when people only
　　　　　Follow powers of soul within themselves.
　　　　　You've overcome this trial, courageously.
　　　　　What once was taken from you, for your good,
　　　　　Will for your good be given you anew.
　　　　　See! Your friend is here! As we have wished:
　　　　　It's she who will receive you in this Temple.

You'll also greet your teacher very soon.
And friends who stand upon the threshold of
Our Temple join with us in the desire
To hail your presence here as knowledge-bringer.

Felix Balde (*To Johannes*)
    Mysticism, through your deed – which always
    Sought the spirit-light on paths within –
    May now be opened up to science too,
    Which only likes to honour sense-existence.

Strader (*To Johannes*)
    For souls who truly strive for spirit-knowledge –
    Though life still keeps them firmly linked to matter –
    For these souls, too, you opened up the paths
    That now can lead them, rightly, to the light.

Johannes   Exalted Master and most noble sirs –
    You all believe you see the man before you
    Who has been able, through his inner trials
    And strength of spirit to create a work
    That's worthy of your praise and to be offered
    Your protection. He, you think, will be
    The one to reconcile, successfully,
    The science of today with age-old, sacred
    Mysticism. And if anything,
    Believe me, other than the voice of my
    Own soul, could give me faith in what I've done,
    Then it would be your words.

Trautmann Our Master's words
    You need not doubt, express but what you feel
    In your own soul. Your inner voice, therefore,
    Will find here all the faith and strength it needs.

Johannes   Oh how I wish that it were so! That I
    Was humbly standing here beseeching that

High favour – that the Temple might bestow
It's blessing on my work. I could believe
In this when I received your word, which made
It known you wished to give my work protection,
And wished to let me step across this threshold,
Which only an initiate can cross.
But on the way, which led me to this place,
A world was opened up to me to which
It is impossible you wished to lead me.
In all his greatness, Ahriman stood there
Before me. Then I learned that he it is
Who fully understands the occult laws
That guide the world. Whatever people think
They know about him counts for nothing. Only
When one's seen him in the spirit can
One understand him. Only Ahriman
Could make me see and feel the horrifying
Truth of my creation. I could see,
Through him, how all the praise of scientists
And critics fails to recognize that the
Creation does not lead a separate life
From its creator. Thus my work will always
Stay connected to me. Thus, although
This work is good and through itself may lead
To good, it's possible that I, from spirit
Realms, may change what I've achieved to evil.
From spirit-lands I'll have to pour
My influence into what shows itself
As consequence of deeds of mine on earth.
And if I let stream evil from the spirit
Worlds into these consequences, then
What's true will cause more harm than error could.
Nor is there any doubt I will in future
Turn to evil all that follows from
My deed. For Ahriman has clearly shown

That what ensues will all belong to him.
When I was hard at work, enthused, enraptured,
Because it led so certainly from step
To step upon the path of truth. I cared
For nothing but the part of me engaged
In research. All the rest of me was left
Untended. Wild desires and impulses
Could grow inside me. What were once just seeds,
When left alone, ran rampant, led their own
Unfettered life and grew to full-blown fruits.
I thought myself in highest spirit-worlds;
But lived in fact in deepest darkness of
The soul. And Ahriman has shown to me,
With brutal clarity, the power of those
Desires and drives – that in the future they'll
Become my very being. Thus I know
What influence I'll wield. Before my book
I'd turned devotedly to Lucifer,
Whose realm I wished to know and understand.
But only now I see what I could not,
When wholly given up to my creation:
That Lucifer surrounded all I thought
In pictures filled with beauty – yet was all
The time creating wild desires. Though dormant
Now, they will in future rule my being.

Trautmann How can someone so far evolved as you
Know all of this so clearly, and yet still
Believe he cannot free himself from evil?
And yet you see what threatens you with ruin…
Destroy it then! Courageously both save
Yourself and all that follows from your deed.
The spirit-pupil must, unflinchingly,
Eradicate what hinders his ascent.

Johannes   I see you're ignorant of higher laws.
What you demand, I could fulfil it now.
And everything you say to me I too
Could tell myself. But karma rules. And what
Today it lets me do, tomorrow it
Will not allow. Yes – things will come to pass
That bring about a dark(e)ning of my spirit.
This can't be helped. I've told you what will be.
And everything in earth or heaven that
Could bring my work an evil consequence
I'll seize on greedily and seek to make
It part of human culture. Ahriman
I then will have to love and give him gladly
All that I've achieved in earthly life.

Pause, during which Johannes ponders deeply.

If all of this concerned myself alone,
I'd keep it in the quietness of my soul.
I would await, in full tranquility,
What lies ahead for me, upon my path.
But it concerns your Brotherhood as badly.
For karma, gradually, will balance out
The evil consequences of my work –
For me and other human souls as well.
The fact that you, though, made so grave an error
Is much more serious for earthly life;
You are the leaders of this life and should
Know how to read within the spirit-worlds,
And therefore you should not have failed to see
This work should have been carried out by someone
Else, and not by me. You should have known
It now must be forgotten – until later
One would come who'd build it up anew –
Who'd have a different influence on their work.
Your judgement – and your lack of it – has stripped

This Brotherhood completely of its right
To stand as leader of this sacred work.
Because my vision shows me this about you,
I have appeared today upon your threshold.
For otherwise I'd never have come near it.
Now that I know this work, that's capable
Of good and harm, can take no blessing here.

Hilary   Dear brothers, friends, what here has been begun
Cannot be taken further at this time.
We must remove ourselves – and go to where
The spirit can make clear to us its will.

Hilary leaves the hall, with Bellicosus, Torquatus and Trautmann. Strader and Felix also leave. Only Johannes and Maria remain where they were. The hall darkens. After a brief pause, the three spirit-figures of Philia, Astrid and Luna appear in a cloud of light, and group themselves in such a way that at first they conceal Maria. What follows is the spiritual experience of Johannes.

Philia   The soul, it is thirsting
To drink of the light
That streams from those worlds
Which an all-caring will
Keeps veiled from mankind.
The spirit is trying
With longing, to listen
To divine conversations,
Which benevolent wisdom
Conceals from the heart.
Thinking that seeks
In regions of soul,
Where far from the senses
The Hidden holds sway,
Is threatened with peril.

Astrid   The souls are expanding
That follow the light

And reach into worlds
Which are opened to Men
By the courage to see.
The spirit is striving
To blessedly live
In divine, godly regions
Which radiant wisdom
Proclaims to the seers.
The hidden, it beckons
To those boldly seeking
The fields high above
Where far from men's thinking
Life's mysteries hide.

Luna

The soul, it is ripening
And fashioning vision,
That springs from those forces
A will that is fearless
Enkindles within us.
From primal foundations
The magical spirits
Gain power of redemption,
Concealed from the senses
By barriers of earth.
And souls that are seeking,
Are following traces
To find those bright doorways
That gods keep locked tight
To a will gone astray.

Voice of Conscience (*invisible*)

Your thoughts are wavering, trembling
On the brink of being's abyss.
All that used to support them you have lost.
And what once would illumine them like the sun
Is blotted out for you.

You go astray in cosmic depths
Which, made drunk with longing,
Men wish to conquer.
You shudder, facing grounds of worlds,
Where all that can give comfort to the soul
Must be abandoned.

The last words pass over immediately into the following words of Maria, who is still concealed by the spirit-figures and is invisible. She speaks at first in a spirit-like voice, but inwardly.

Maria   Incline your soul, therefore,
Towards the powers of love,
Which once could permeate your hope
With living warmth,
Which once could shine into your will
Their spirit-light.
Rescue out of loneliness
The seeking forces of your heart –
And feel the nearness of your friend
Amidst the darknesses you strive through.

The spirit-figures and the cloud of light disappear. Maria becomes visible at the place where she had been previously. The experience from now on returns to the physical plane.

Johannes (*out of deep contemplation*)
Where have I been? The forces of my soul
Unveiled to me my whirling inner chaos;
The conscience of the world revealed to me
What I have lost; there sounded then, amidst
The darkness, blessing me, the voice of love.

Maria   Johannes, the companion of your soul
May once again be present at your side;
And she may follow you to depths of worlds,
Where souls attain the feeling of the Gods,

Through shattering inner victories that destroy,
And boldly from destruction win back being.
And through the endless empty fields of ice
She's gained the right to lead her friend, where he'll
Attain that light, which spirits must create
When darknesses may lame the powers of life.
My friend, you stand upon that threshold
Where everything one has achieved
One has to lose. You often gained a glimpse
Of spirit-worlds, and drew from this the strength
Which made you capable of your creation.
And this creation now seems lost to you.
Don't demand that this be otherwise.
To do so would just rob from you all strength
To find your further way into the spirit.
Whether you walk in paths of truth or error
You'll always hold the doorway open,
Through which your soul may take its rightful steps,
If you can learn to bear courageously
Necessities that spring from spirit-realms.
This is the law of spirit-pupilship.
As long as you can entertain the wish
That what has happened to you might be
Different, you'll lack the strength that's needed
To uphold yourself in spirit worlds.
That you have lost what has been won by you
Enables you to know how rightly to
Transform your spirit-path in future.
That understanding you have always used
To judge your actions, from this moment on
You can no longer call on, if indeed
In utter earnestness you know it lost.
Your being, therefore, must become completely
Silent – and await in silence what
The spirit brings; and only be your guide

Again, when you have won yourself anew.
Often you have met the solemn Guardian
Who keeps stern watch upon the threshold,
Separating worlds of sense from spirit-being;
But never yet have you gone past him.
Always at his gaze did you turn back
And only from the outside saw that world. –
You have not been *within* that spirit-world
Spread out around you; now, though, be prepared
For all that will reveal itself to you,
When you are not just able to *approach*,
But also, by my side, to *cross* the threshold.

Curtain.

Scene Three

In Lucifer's realm. A space not bound by artificial walls, but by plant-like and animal-like forms and by other strange, fantastical forms. To the left is the throne of Lucifer. There are present, to begin with, the soul of Capesius and Maria.

Maria

> You, who's known to me, within the realm
> Of sense-existence, as Capesius
> Why here, in Lucifer's domain, are you
> The being I meet first? There's danger just
> To breathe the air the Regent Spirit breathes here.

Capesius

> Don't speak to me about Capesius.
> Who once, upon the earth, struggled through
> A life he long since saw but as a dream.
> He fixed his mind on what took place within
> The stream of time. He thought he would discover,
> Thus, the forces that give rise to human
> Cultural life, and all that flows from it.
> His soul attempted to retain all that
> It knew about these forces. But from this
> Realm here, it's possible to view the knowledge
> He was cultivating then. He thought
> He grasped true images, that could have opened
> Up realities; but seen from here
> It is quite clear they are but idle dreams
> That spirits weave into weak souls on earth.
> For people cannot bear reality.
> What fear and dire confusion they would feel
> If they were able to experience
> How spirits guide the stream of all existence.

Maria

> You speak as I have only heard those speak
> Who never yet were incarnate on earth.
> Such beings say that earth-life has no meaning –
> And matters little in the Universe,

But those belonging to the realm of earth
Who know they owe it thanks for their best forces,
Must hold a very different opinion.
They value many threads of destiny
That join the earthly and the cosmic worlds.
Even Lucifer, so powerful here,
Keeps his gaze quite fixed upon the earth,
And seeks to guide men's deeds in such a way
His spirit then may pluck their ripened fruits.
He knows that if he found no spoils upon
The earth, he soon would fall to darkness. So
His destiny depends on it as well.
It's like this too for other cosmic beings.
And when, in image, we behold the goals
That Lucifer is striving for, and then
Compare these with the goals of Powers to whom
He stands in opposition – we may know
That Lucifer can best be thwarted through
The victories we gain over ourselves.

Capesius   The person who converses with you here
Finds those times quite dreadful when he's forced
To wrap his body round him, which still lives,
And which has kept its earthly form, although
The spirit can no longer master it.
At times like these the spirit feels the worlds
That he most highly treasures are collapsing.
It seems a narrow cruel prison shuts
Him in, whose bars look out on nothingness.
All memory of his life is blotted out.
He often feels the people round about him
But cannot understand the things they say.
He grasps but certain words, which rise above
Their speech, and these make him remember all
The beauty he may see in spirit-worlds.

He is and isn't then within his body.
To see his life in it, from here, brings fear.
And all that he can do is crave the moment
Freeing him completely from that body.

Maria   The body that belongs to souls on earth,
Bears the means, through images sublime,
To recreate, within itself, divine beauty.
These images, though their existence
In the soul appears but shadow-like,
Are nonetheless the seeds, which as the world
Evolves, must one day blossom and bear fruit.
And we only perceive the true sense of
Our lives of soul, when in our bodies there
Is felt the strength that leads towards the real 'I'.

Capesius   O do not speak this word, before the being
Who now appears to you in spirit-realms,
And who on earth lives as Capesius.
When that word sounds, that burns him in this place
Like fire, he'd like to flee.

Maria   So do you hate
The very thing that gives humanity
True being? If this word causes you such fear
How can you live within this realm? For nobody
Could even reach this place who can't
Experience the being of this word.

Capesius   The one before you here has often stood
In front of Lucifer, who rules this realm.
And Lucifer could then reveal to him
That human souls, who can use consciously
The strength arising from their earthly bodies,
Only bring great harm into the kingdom
That obeys his will – whereas those souls
Who live quite powerlessly within their bodies,

And yet have spirit-sight – these merely learn
In Lucifer's domain and cannot harm it.

Maria   I know that one can only learn through vision
In this spirit-realm and not through words.
What vision has revealed to me just now
Through your appearing here the way you have,
Will prove a strong step forward for my soul
Upon its path of spirit-pupilship.

Capesius   But one receives not only teachings in
This place. One also faces *duties* here.
You have conversed here with a being, whose name
Whilst in his body is Capesius.
The spirit-glimpses you have had into
Your previous lives on earth reveal that through
Your karma you are much in debt to him;
You therefore must approach Lord Lucifer
And ask the radiant bearer of the Light
Permission to protect Capesius
On earth. You'll know, in your great wisdom,
What you can do for him, so that he's led
To you again, in later life on earth,
And then, through you, the debt may be erased.

Maria   Should I then let this duty, which I deem
So sacred, be fulfilled through Lucifer?

Capesius   You will, of course, wish to fulfil this duty.
And only Lucifer can help you do so.
But look – he's here himself – the Lord of Light.

Capesius leaves. Lucifer appears and, during the course of his speech, Benedictus.

Lucifer   Maria, you desire before my throne
To win self-knowledge for that human soul
To whom you stand so near in earthly life.
But only through his gazing on my being

Will he, in truth, gain knowledge of himself.
He does not need your help to come to this.
How could you possibly believe that I
Would grant what you are seeking for your friend?
You still name Benedictus as your teacher.
He is my great opponent on the earth,
Who to my enemies devotes his strength.
He has already snatched from me too much.
Johannes, though, has separated from him –
And has made me, instead, his guide and teacher.
Because he lacks still full clairvoyant vision,
He cannot yet behold my truest being;
Later, though, through me, he will achieve this –
And when he does – he will be wholly mine.
But you I order not to speak a word
In any way referring to Johannes,
As long as you remain before my throne.
A single word like this would burn me here.
For words are deeds within this place, and from
Them, further deeds will have to follow.
But what would have to follow from your words –
That may not be!

Benedictus   You *have* to hear her. For
Where someone's words possess the power of deeds
This is the consequence of former deeds.
The deeds already have been done, that force
You, Lucifer, to now obey her will.
Maria, you'll know, is my true spirit-pupil –
Whom I could lead up to that point where she
Could recognize her highest spirit-duty –
Which she will carry out unswervingly.
By carrying out this duty, she will form,
Within Johannes, healing forces, which
Will have the power to free him from your realm.

Maria bears a sacred, solemn vow
Within her, which, in the evolving world,
Can quicken into life such healing forces.
You soon will even hear this vow in words;
But if, through strength of thought, you'd dim, for once,
Your radiant body of light, which gives
You all your magic power to oppose
And gain control of every form of selfhood,
You'll surely hear this vow's resplendent healing.
This will become so strong in future, that
Its force of love will powerfully draw
Johannes into its own realm.

Maria
Johannes will appear within this place.
But not just in that customary form
That souls consider as their own.
There will appear as well that other being
That humans bear within them, unobserved –
That stronger, truer likeness of themselves.
Johannes, if he only recognized
You, as he knows you in his earthly form,
Would not gain everything he needs to take
His rightful steps upon his path of soul.
So you must grant unto his stronger likeness –
That powerful living image of himself –
What he will need upon those spirit-paths
On which I'll have to lead him in the future.

Lucifer
Johannes, then, must now appear to me?
I feel indeed the power that you wield.
It has opposed me since the world began.

Johannes and his etheric likeness – or double – appear from opposite sides.

Johannes
I face you once again, my likeness, mirror-
Image. Always you've appeared before
So that I've had to look with horror on

Myself. I understand you still but little.
And yet I know it's you that guides my soul.
You are the block and hindrance to my freedom.
You are the reason too I cannot grasp
What in reality I am. I need
To hear you speak in front of Lucifer
To see what I must still achieve in future.

The Double   It's true that many times already I've
Appeared before Johannes, bringing him
To know himself. I only worked, though, in
His silent depths, still hidden, even now,
From what he knows. But then, some time ago,
My whole existence changed, transformed, within him.
Maria, years before, stood by his side –
He felt himself at one with her, in spirit;
I showed to him his soul in fact was led
By unacknowledged passion and desire.
He understood this just as accusation.
But you, exalted bearer of the light,
Showed sensuality the way to place
Itself in service of the spirit. From
Mari(a) Johannes had to separate.
Since then he sought the discipline of thought,
Which has the power to purge and heal the soul.
And all that streamed, like light, from his pure thinking,
Poured also into me. I was transformed.
His purity I feel in me as well.
He has no cause to fear me if he now
Feels drawn towards Maria. But, he's still
Held bound within your kingdom. Lucifer,
Release him! In this hour I call him back.
He's able to experience my being
And you will not determine what this means.
He needs me now, so that his thinking's joined

By warmth of soul and strength of heart, which now
May truly come to birth within him. Through me
He must win back his full humanity.

Lucifer   Your striving's good. But in the way you wish –
Impossible! If I would give you to
Johannes in that form which years ago
You showed to him, he very soon would offer
All his love to thought and pale, cold knowledge;
The warm and personal self in him would seem
Unfeeling, void and as if it were dead.
My powers can never serve to make him thus.
Experiencing me he shall discover
Personality and life of self.
You I now must change, transform, for his
Own good, and so he now develops rightly.
For ages now I have prepared what will
Appear in you so clearly. You will show
Yourself in future as a different being.
Johannes will no longer love Maria
As in past ages he has done. But *love*
He will, with all the overpowering strength
Of passion he experienced for her.

Benedictus You wish to change the work of beauty that
We have achieved, and make it serve your ends.
You once could bind Johannes to you, through
His strength of heart; but now you see you'll need
To bind him even tighter in your chains,
If you're to keep his being as your own.
Johannes seeks his rightful path –
To let his heart entirely obey his spirit.
If he succeeds, the deed of knowledge that
He has accomplished on the earth, would have,
In future, to be given to those powers
That you have fought against since earth began.

If you succeed, through cunning, to transform
The love Johannes felt towards Maria,
Into the passion that your aims require,
Then he indeed, from out the spirit-worlds,
Will change the good he could achieve to evil.

Maria   Then things can still be saved? And it is not
Decreed Johannes *must* succumb unto
Those powers wishing to usurp his deed?

Benedictus   If all the forces stay as they have been
Till now, then, yes, he would succumb. But if
At the propitious moment, you allow
Your vow to take effect within your soul,
Then this will greatly change things in the future.

Lucifer   Then work, compelling powers
And elemental spirits, feel
The power of your master.
Make straight the path
Along which can be led
Away from bounds of earth
Into bright Lucifer's domain
All that my wishes crave
And that must be obedient to my will.

Theodora (*appears*)
Who calls me here? This realm is strange to me.
I know love only when the worlds of gods
Reveal themselves with love within my soul –
When warmth, which weaves its blessing in my heart,
Enables me to speak true spirit-words.

Johannes' Double
I feel how you transform my whole existence
You have appeared and I am one who can
Do nothing now unless you fill my being.

Through me Johannes will belong to you.
From now on he will turn to you that love,
That once sprang from his heart towards Maria,
So tremblingly and with such glowing fire within.
He saw you years ago but did not feel,
Back then, how deep within his soul there stirred
In him, unconsciously, the warmth of love.
This now will surge to life within him, and
Completely fill his being with that power
That makes him turn his thoughts to you alone.

Benedictus   The rightful moment fast approaches us.
Lucifer has now let loose his strongest
Power. Maria, your inner path of soul,
With all its might, must stand against him now.

Maria   You, who bears that light that always wants
To make love only serve one's self alone,
When earth began, you gave weak humans knowledge,
When they had first been destined by the gods,
Without their own self-will, unconsciously
To follow what the spirit willed. Since then
Each human soul has been the stage on which
You've never ceased to battle with the gods.
Already, though, the times are nearing, which
Must bring defeat to you and to your realm.
A bold, courageous thinker has now found
The way to free all knowledge from your gifts,
So that it can devote itself instead
To all the truest gods of humankind.
Because Johannes, by what he has done,
Has freed that fruit of knowledge from your grasp,
Through which you tempted humankind, you wish
To tempt him now, though love, which in his plan
Of destiny, he shouldn't ever feel
For Theodora. You desire, with love,

To fight with wisdom; just as once, with wisdom,
You sought to fight with love. But know that in
The heart, with which Maria now confronts
You, lives the strength, acquired by her spirit-
Pupilship, to always keep self-love
Away from knowledge. Never will I feel
From this time forth, that bliss that people feel
When thoughts grow ripe. My heart's prepared
To serve in sacrifice – through which my spirit
Will only ever think in such a way
That offers to the Gods the fruits of knowledge.
Knowledge will become for me an act
Of service. What I shall achieve through this
Will powerfully stream into Johannes.
And when within his heart in future he
Will often hear your words: "The human being
Can only find in *love* what makes him strong",
His heart itself will powerfully reply:
You offered to mankind, when earth began,
The fruits of *wisdom* – which they gladly ate.
The fruits of *love*, though – they must only let
Themselves receive – when offered by the gods.

Lucifer   Then I will fight!

Brief darkness

Benedictus   And fighting serve the gods!

Thunder.
Curtain.

Scene Four

A room whose main colour is rose-red. It belongs to the home of Strader and Theodora, his wife. From the way the furniture is arranged, one can see that Theodora and Strader carry on different kinds of work in this room that they share. On his desk there are models of machines; on hers things that have to do with mysticism. The two of them are in conversation, in which they contemplate, together, their seventh wedding anniversary.

Strader   It's seven years, to the day, that you
Became the dear companion of my life
And the source of light, illuminating
An existence, which, before, only
Darkness always threatened to approach.
I was a man so poor in spirit, when
You joined me by my side and gave me what
The world, till then, had kept away from me.
For many years I had been trying to
Discover, strictly scientifically,
Life's values and the purpose of existence.
But one day I was forced to recognize
That these attempts were all completely futile.
Through you I could perceive, quite clearly, how
The spirit seeks to show itself in someone,
And how it can reveal those things that had
Escaped my knowledge and my powers of thinking.
Upon that day I saw you in the group
Of people that was led by Benedictus.
And I could listen to your revelation.
Then later, in Johannes, I could not
But recognize the strong effects of spirit-
Pupilship within a human soul.
What I experienced through all of this
Robbed me of my faith in science and reason.
And yet could show me nothing at that time

That could have brought me any understanding.
I wanted nothing more to do with thinking,
I wanted just to spend my life in dullness;
My life seemed not worth living any more.
And then I lived a tortured, bleak existence
Until I met you for the second time.
And soon, this time, we both became close friends.

Theodora   I so well understand how on this day
Your memory can bring before your soul
So livingly the life of former times.
My heart – it also feels the need today
To gaze back to that time when we both met,
And with such blessing joined our lives together.
That was the time I always felt that power
Strenthening, that made me able to
Receive true knowledge from the spirit-worlds.
And under Felix Balde's special guidance
This power could ripen in me to the height
At which it stood then, seven years ago.
Around that time I met Capesius
In Felix Balde's lonely woodland cottage.
After all his years of research, he
Had struggled through to spirit-pupilship.
He really wanted now to get to know
My kind of vision into spirit-worlds.
I'd meet him very often after that.
And in his house I then met you – and I
Could bring your suffering mind some healing.

Strader   And then my soul received true light, that for
So long had just been gazing into darkness.
I saw now what the spirit really is.
You let me recognize, so perfectly,
Your revelations from the spirit-worlds,
That all my doubts just vanished – disappeared.

The overwhelming way this worked on me
Was such that I, at first, could only see
In you the mediator of the spirit.
It needed longer till I recognized
That more than just my spirit listened to
The words unveiling to it its true home;
My heart as well was given to the speaker
And could not manage now without her nearness.

Theodora Then you confided in me what you felt.
It was so very strange, the way you spoke.
It was as if it was impossible for you
To form a single thought that maybe all
The longing in your heart might be fulfilled.
That's how your words all sounded – asking but
A true friend of your soul for some advice.
You spoke about your needing help from me,
And also how, to face your troubled state,
You needed such great strengthening in soul.

Strader That you, my spirit-messenger, could be
Ordained by destiny to be my wife,
Was very far away from all my thoughts
When, seeking help, I opened up to you.

Theodora And then the words I could not help but utter –
Words the heart itself had set free from
The heart – that it could not be otherwise.
For hearts must often show our destiny.

Strader And then – when there was uttered from your heart
Those words of destiny – great waves of life
Streamed throughout my soul, which at the time
I could not feel, which only later rose
In memory from deep within the soul
And then were felt as rays of healing light.
And I could fully know all I remembered,

Though I had not experienced it, for I
Was far, as yet, from apprehending spirit.
That was the first time I had ever known
The spirit shine directly in my soul.
That has not ever been repeated, yet
It filled me with such inner certainty
That brightly will illumine all my days.
And this led on to seven beautiful years.
And I have come to feel how even the
Mechanical technology I serve
Can let itself be fructified by souls
Who can relate directly to the spirit.
It was that spirit-power alone, you gave
In such abundance, that enabled me
To so perceive the interplay of forces,
That, like something given, suddenly
That creation stood before my spirit
From which, indeed, so much can now be hoped.
Within the light you shone, my soul could feel
Its forces growing into fullness, which
Would just have withered, had it lived alone.
The certainty in life that I had gained
Became so strong, I still remained myself
And upright when, so shatteringly, Johannes
Damned his own accomplishment in knowledge
Before the Rosicrucians, and pronounced
Against himself such harsh, condemning judgement,
In the very hour that could have brought
Him to the pinnacle of his whole life.
I still maintained my inner certainty
When the outer world appeared to show
To me an endless sea of contradictions.
And all of this I gained through you alone.
The revelations of the spirit I
Received from you, first brought me long-sought knowledge.

And when those revelations came no more
You still remained my source of strength and light.

Theodora (*as a broken sentence, in deep thought*)
And then the revelations came no more…

Strader   It's this that's often been of grave concern
To me. I've wondered if, perhaps, you suffered
Deeply from your loss of seership,
But to spare me, never spoke of this;
And yet your equanimity revealed
You bore, quite calmly, all that life had brought.
It's only recently that you have changed;
The radiance of joy does not surround
You now; your eyes' soft glowing light is fading.

Theodora   That my spirit-revelations left me
Did not pain me. Destiny had changed
My path – and I accepted this quite calmly.
They have returned. This is my agony.

Strader   Theodora, now, for the first time, in all
These seven years, I cannot understand you.
Your vision of the spirit-worlds has always
Been for you a source of inner blessing.

Theodora   Quite different are the revelations now.
At first, just like before, I feel compelled
To dampen down completely my own thinking;
But whereas, previously, when I'd become
A silent, empty vessel, waiting, soon
There wove around my soul a gentle light,
And then the spirit-images appeared,
There now is born, instead, an unquiet feeling,
Of something, yes, unseen, and yet I know
This power I feel assails me from outside.
And through my inner world there floods such fear

              I can't throw off – it takes control of me.
And all I want to do is flee that being –
Invisible, and yet abhorrent, vile.
It moves towards me, overflowing with
Desire, so I must hate that revelation.

Strader   I cannot see how this is possible
With Theodora. Such experiences,
Normally, are seen but to reflect
What is at work in one's own soul. But your
Soul could not ever show itself like this.

Theodora (*painfully, slowly, in deep thought*)
              I know. I'm all too well aware of this.
And so, with all the strength my soul could muster,
I sank myself, devotedly, into
The world of spirits, and implored those beings
Who previously inclined to me so often,
To show me, through their grace, how I
Could find the causes of my suffering.
(*Broken words follow*)
              And there… it was… that shape of light… again…
It formed… into the image… of a man…
I clearly saw… Johannes…

Strader (*painfully, overcome by a sudden inrush of feelings*)
              What? Johannes...
The man in whom I always put my faith.
             - - - - - - - - - - -
Pause, then in painful reflection.

              When I now summon up before my soul…
The way that he opposed the Brotherhood…
His words about himself and Ahriman…

Theodora sinks into her thoughts and gazes into emptiness, as if her spirit is completely absent.

              O Theodora… now what do you see?

                    Curtain.

Scene Five

A room in the woodland cottage which, in 'The Trial of the Soul' was seen as the Baldes' home. There are present: Felicia Balde, Felix Balde, Capesius, Strader.

Frau Balde   And so we may not feel again the radiant
Beauty of her being till we ourselves
Enter the world that has now taken her
Away from us before her time. A few
Short weeks ago we still experienced
So thankfully, the gentle mildness, which
So warmly breathed through every word she spoke.

Felix   My wife, Felicia and I, both loved
Her from our deepest, inmost soul.
We therefore understand your grief and sorrow.

Strader   Beloved Theodora, yes, she spoke
Of Frau Felicia and father Felix
Even in the last hours of her life.
She also knew so intimately all
That life can bring you here from day to day.

I have to find my way then on my own.
She was the ground and meaning of my life.
All she gave can never die for me,
And yet – she is not here.

Felix   With you
We lovingly will send our thoughts towards
Her in the spirit-worlds and we will be
United with her once again in future.
And yet I have to say: it was a very
Great surprise to hear her life had ended.
For there was formed in me, over the years
A vision, which, at certain moments, quite

Unsought, will show me people's inner power
Of life. This vision, though, with her, misled me.
I really only ever could believe
That Theodora still for years, on earth,
Would give that love which has brought so much help
To many people, both in joy and sorrow.

Strader   It's very strange the way it all happened.
Her mood, through everything, since I have known her,
Was always one of perfect health and balance.
Only since she first became aware
That something, unknown, haunted her, desiring
To be near her, did a sense of gloom
Increasingly take hold of her,
And suffering then streamed throughout her being.
And one could see how what she battled with,
Within, consumed the forces of her body.
When through my worry I would weigh upon
Her, with the questions that I asked, she said
She felt quite at the mercy of those kind
Of thoughts, which rouse up fears and work like fire.
When, through powers of thought, she ventured to
Behold the cause of all her suffering,
Always to her spirit-eye appeared…
Johannes… who we both esteemed so highly.
Yet this impression always left her with
A powerful feeling, telling her quite clearly
That, from now on, she must fear Johannes.

Capesius   It is the stern decree of destiny
That Theodora and Johannes should
Not ever meet, within this life, in passion.
If one of them has feelings for the other
That are not grounded in the spirit alone,
They set themselves against the laws of worlds.
Johannes violates, within his heart,

The strict command of powers of destiny:
He should not direct to Theodora
Thoughts, within his soul, which cause her harm.
He feels, though, all that he should never feel.
And through this opposition, he is forming,
Even now, those forces, which, in future,
May deliver him to powers of darkness.
Theodora, driven by force, against
Her will to Lucifer, experienced
Unconsciously the Lord of Light then fill
Johannes full of sensual passion for her.
Theodora and Maria – to whom
Johannes is entrusted in the spirit –
Found themselves, within the selfsame moment,
In the realm so hostile to the gods.
It was intended that Johannes should
Be separated from Maria and through
False powers of love be bound to Lucifer.
What Theodora thus endured in soul
Became in her an all-consuming fire,
Which working onwards brought her sufferings.

Strader   Please tell me, Father Felix, what this means.
           Capesius speaks so riddlingly of things
           My soul cannot begin to understand,
           And yet still finds appalling, horrible.

Felix   Capesius, through those inner paths of soul
           He felt himself compelled to walk upon,
           Has gradually been driven ever further
           Into his own remark(a)ble spirit-world.
           His spirit lives in higher worlds
           Completely disregarding all those things
           Which speak to people through their earthly senses.
           He carries out as if by habit only
           Everything he used to do in life.

He keeps on visiting his friends, and even
Spends longs hours with them, although, while near
Them, he seems far away, within himself.
However, what he sees in spirit, this
Has always been correct, each time that I
Have tested it through my own soul research.
In this case too, therefore, I have to state
My own belief, that on his paths in spirit,
He has indeed received into his soul
The truth of Theodora's destiny.

Felicia   It is so very strange, he pays no heed
At all to conversations people
Have around him; and his soul, released
From its connection with the body, seems
As if it only gazed on spirit-worlds.
But certain words affect him nonetheless,
And draw him back from his great isolation,
And then he tells of things in spirit-realms
Which seem, somehow, connected to this world.
At other times, whatever one may say
In front of him, it seems one has said nothing.

Strader   But if he spoke the truth – how dreadful – monstrous!

Theodora's soul appears.

Theodora's soul
Capesius has been permitted to
Gain knowledge of my being within the world
I now inhabit. Everything that he
Has spoken here is true. Johannes, though,
Despite all that has happened, must not be
Allowed to fall. Maria in her heart
Has lit the flame of sacrificial love;
And Theodora will, from spirit-heights,
Send blessing rays of strong and healing love.

She makes a gesture of blessing.

Felix   You must remain completely calm, dear Strader.
           She wants to speak with you. I understand
           The signs that she is giving us; so listen.

Theodora (*who has made a movement with her hands towards Strader*)
           Johannes has clairvoyant powers: and thus
           He'll find me even in the spirit-realms.
           He must not do so until he's prepared
           To look for me, completely free of passion.
           In future he will also need your help.
           I entreat you now: please give him this.

Strader   O my Theodora! You still turn
           Towards me, even now, with healing love!
           Just say then what it is you wish to happen.

           Theodora makes a sign towards Capesius.

Felix Balde She shows that she can speak no more. She wishes
             Us to listen to Capesius.

           Theodora disappears.

Capesius   Johannes, when he wishes to make use
           Of spirit-eyes, can still see Theodora.
           And not even her death itself therefore,
           Will kill the harmful passion that he feels.
           All he will need to do is act in other
           Ways than he has done when Theodora
           Still was living in her earthly body;
           His passion now will strive towards the light
           That can reveal itself to her from spirit-
           Heights, although she has no earthly knowledge.
           Johannes is to seize that light, so that
           Through him, it may be won by Lucifer.
           Then, through the light of gods, could Lucifer

Keep held within his realm, throughout long ages
Of eternity, the science that
Johannes has attained through earthly forces.
For Lucifer, since earth itself began,
Has always looked for those who have attained,
Through false desires, the wisdom of the gods.
He wishes now to bring together purest
Spiritual vision with human knowledge, which
Would thereby change itself from good to bad.
Johannes, though, will certainly be brought
To leave his evil paths if Strader can
Direct himself to goals which can, in future,
Spiritually transform our human knowledge,
And thus approach the knowledge of the gods.
Strader must, if he's to know these goals,
Now turn to Benedictus, as a pupil.

     Pause.

Strader   Dear Felix, help me understand. Can it
Be true Capesius was bidden to
Reveal these things to me by Theodora?

Felix   In recent times I've very often held
Most earnest counsel with my inner being
To gain illumination on this man.
I'll happily confide all that I know.
Capesius is undergoing true
And rightful spirit-pupilship, though his
Behaviour might make it seem otherwise.
It is laid down, within his destiny,
That one day he will carry out great tasks
In spiritual life and in the life of culture.
He only can fulfil these if his spirit,
Even now, prepares itself for them.
His being, though, was also much inclined,

Instead of seeing light on spirit-paths,
To dedicate itself to that false science
By which so many souls are blinded now.
The stern-faced Guardian at the solemn Threshold,
Between this world of sense and spirit-worlds,
Had quite unusually strict demands
When, finally, Capesius reached that Portal.
To the man whose search had been so earnest,
The doorway had to open, but be then
Immediately shut again behind him.
Had this not happened, through the way that he
Had previously acquired his forces, while
In sense-existence, he would then have not,
In spirit-realms, made any further progress.
The way that he can best prepare himself,
For that high service he will have to carry
Out in future, is to pay the present
Time no heed, and let it pass him by.

Felicia
To only one thing still does he pay heed.
The fairy tales that I so often told him;
He drank them in and always felt them like
A deep refreshing draught, that could renew
His thinking and refill his empty soul.

Capesius
Fairy tales can also reach the sprit-realms,
If you can also tell them in the spirit.

Felicia
Then every time that I compose myself
And speak my tales with my inner being,
I'll think of you with love, so that they may
Be heard by you as well, in spirit-realms.

Curtain.

Scene Six

A space which is not bound by artificial walls, but which is surrounded by inter-twining, tree-like plants and shapes, which spread out and send shoots into the interior space. As a result of natural processes the whole place is in wild motion and at times filled with storms. At the beginning of the scene, Capesius and Maria are on stage.

Benedictus (*as yet only audible, not visible*)
>Within your thinking, cosmic thoughts are living.

Capesius
>The noble voice of Benedictus. Here
>His words resound in spirit-tones. The same
>As those which in his book of life he's written
>For his pupils; hard to grasp and harder
>To experience. Where in spirit-worlds is this,
>Where words resound that challenge souls on earth?

Maria
>You've wandered in the spirit world so long
>In such a way that much has been revealed;
>And yet you do not recognize this realm?

Capesius
>I easily understand how here a being
>Communicates its deep, essential self
>Not through itself, but through all else around.
>The whole is full of light even when the part
>Alone is often dark. But when what here
>Exists desires to actively create
>With beings of the earth, the soul begins to lose
>Its understanding. Not the part alone,
>The whole as well is often shrouded then
>In deepest darkness. Why there should reecho
>Here the words that Benedictus wrote
>For souls on earth makes all that happens here
>A riddle.

Benedictus (*still invisible*)
        Within your feeling cosmic powers are weaving.

Capesius   Another saying of Benedictus given
        To people on earth! Said here in his own voice.
        It streams, and so gives rise to darkness
        Through this region's limitless expanse.

Maria   I feel already what must be experienced
        Here, amidst this region's endless distance.
        Benedictus, close, is calling me.
        He wants to show to me, within this place,
        What even souls discipled to the light
        Can never grasp, when joined to worlds of sense.
        They must be able to seek out their teacher
        In those places where he does not just
        Coin words, in language, indicating beings,
        But where he can calls forth the living script
        Which speaks with world-wide meaning to the soul.
        I will release my inner being from earth-
        Existence, and await what wills to be
        Revealed from spirit-worlds; and when I turn
        Again towards the earth, this will, as thought,
        Shine forth its knowing light within my soul.

Benedictus (*appearing from the background*)
        Attain yourself in cosmic powers of thought,
        And lose yourself through life of cosmic powers;
        And you will find, through you, the goals of earth,
        Reflecting bright within the cosmic light.

Capesius   Benedictus, in the spirit, now
        Is even here himself – not just his words.
        Does then the spirit-teacher bear his earthly
        Knowledge, livingly, to spirit-places?
        And what do these words mean, when uttered here,
        Which work quite differently in earthly life?

Benedictus   Capesius, during the times you spent
             On earth, you came into my circle, though
             You never consciously became my pupil.

Capesius   Capesius is not here in this place;
             And nor does his soul wish to hear of him.

Benedictus   You have no wish to feel yourself within
             Capesius. But you, in memory,
             Should gaze upon him, spiritually.
             It was the strong and active power of thinking
             That unveiled for you the life of spirit.
             And then your soul-life freed itself from thinking's
             Shifting play of dreams within the body.
             It felt itself too weak to journey with him out
             Of cosmic distances to depths of soul.
             Too strong only to look with him through darknesses
             Of earth on light-filled spirit-heights.
             I must accompany whoever has
             Received the spirit-light from me on earth,
             Whether they became my spirit-pupil
             Knowingly or just unconsciously.
             And I must guide them further on the paths
             That they, through me, set out on in the spirit.
             Your seeing soul that finds itself in cosmic
             Distances, has learned to near the spirit.
             For you can follow it, freed from your body.
             But you cannot behold, as yet, quite
             Free from thought, the true being, in spirit-realms.
             You can lay by the body of the senses,
             But not the fine-spun body of your thinking.
             The world in its true form you'll only see,
             When nothing tied to your own being remains,
             To cloud for you true clarity of sight.
             For only those who've learned to see their thinking
             From outside, the way clairvoyant powers

See the body, once set free from it,
Can enter full realities of spirit.
See therefore, in images, that powers
Of seership may then transform to knowledge,
Thoughts, that take on form, like living beings,
Beheld in space, that mirror human thinking.

A soft, friendly light begins shining. The soul forces, Philia, Astrid and Luna enter in a luminous cloud. Capesius and Maria leave.

Chorus of Soul Forces (Philia, Astrid and Luna)
Now thoughts hover near
Like weaving of dreams
Arising as beings
Essential to souls;
Self-fashioning will,
Self-wakening feeling,
Self-mastering thinking,
Emerge for the dreamer.

As these words are sounding, Lucifer enters on one side and Ahriman on the other. They take their places on either side of the space.

Lucifer (*expansively, emphasising every word*)
Within your willing cosmic beings are working.

From Lucifer's side, beings move forward, representing thoughts. They carry out dance-like movements which portray the thought-forms corresponding to Lucifer's words.

Ahriman   The cosmic beings are confusing you.

After these words, thought-Beings appear from Ahriman's side, carrying out dance movements that correspond, as forms, to his words. Afterwards the movements of both groups are carried out together.

Lucifer   Within your feeling cosmic powers are weaving.

The thought beings on Lucifer's side repeat their movements.

Ahriman   The cosmic powers are misleading you.

The thought beings on Ahriman's side repeat their movements; then both move again together.

Lucifer   Within your thinking cosmic thoughts are living.

Repetition of the movements by Lucifer's group.

Ahriman   The cosmic thoughts are leading you astray.

Repetition of the movements by Ahriman's group.
     Then the movements are repeated four times – each group, separately, one time, and three times together.
     The thought-beings disappear to left and right. Lucifer and Ahriman remain. Philia, Astrid and Luna appear from the background, and speak the same words as before, slightly altered.

Chorus of Soul Forces (Philia, Astrid and Luna)
          So thoughts hovered near
          Like weaving of dreams
          Arising as beings
          Essential to souls;
          Self-fashioning will,
          Self-wakening feeling,
          Self-mastering thinking,
          Emerged for the dreamer.

Philia, Astrid and Luna disappear. Capesius re-enters. After he has spoken a few words, Maria appears – who is at first invisible to him.

Capesius   The way the soul experiences itself
          Is inwardly; it feels itself within.
          The soul believes that it does think, because
          It sees no thoughts spread out in space before it.
          And it believes it feels, for feelings don't
          Shine out, like lightnings flashing from the clouds.
          It sees the worlds of space and looking up
          Beholds the clouds above... if this was not

The way it was: if lightnings flashed, and yet
There were no eyes to see them – the soul would then
Believe the lightning was within itself.
The soul does not see Lucifer, from whom
Our thoughts all spring and all our feelings flow;
So it believes that these are ours alone.
Why does it submit to such delusion?
O soul – give yourself the answer... but...
From where? From you? Don't even try... Perhaps
The answer too... would not be yours... would be...
From Lucifer...

Maria   But even were this so –
Is that a reason not to seek? Descend
Into the depths to find the answer.

Capesius   How can a being hear my inmost soul?

Maria   No soul is separate here. Only the body
Brings us separation. Here in words
The other speaks, each one can hear themselves.
And so you only tell yourself, when I
Tell you: to seek the answer in the depths.

Capesius   But in the depths... there threatens dreadful... fear.

Maria   Yes, for certain it is there! But ask
Yourself, once you have pressed into its realm,
If it may not reveal itself quite clearly.
Ask Lucifer if it Is he, who pours
This fear into the weakness of your soul.

Lucifer   All those who flee me love me. Children of
The earth have never ceased to love me, though they
Feel they shouldn't. All my deeds they seek.
In frigid forms of truth they would be starved
Throughout long ages of the earth, did I
Not drop the pearl of beauty in their souls

> To brighten up their pale existence. Into
> Artists' souls, especially, stream my powers.
> Whatever human beings have ever seen
> As beauty springs from me and finds its
> Archetype within my realm. So ask yourself
> If I am one you'd ever need to fear.

Maria

> Fear is a stranger in the land of light.
> It is desire that Lucifer inspires,
> Not fear – which comes from quite another realm.

Ahriman

> I was a god, an equal of the gods.
> Till they curtailed my ancient rights, I wished
> To shape men so for Lucifer that each
> Would be a world unto themselves. As Lucifer
> Would be example only, not
> A ruler, I desired to give all men
> The strength to prove the like of Lucifer.
> And had I stayed within the realms of gods
> That would have been the case when earth began.
> The gods, though, wished to be the lords on earth,
> And so they had to banish from their realms
> My strength, and bind it in the subterranean
> Depths, in case I gave men too much power.
> And so only from here – from the abyss
> Can I send out my forceful strength to men
> On earth; but on the way – it turns – *to fear.*

During Ahriman's final words, Benedictus appears.

Capesius

> Whoever hears what each of these two powers
> Has spoken out into the widths of worlds –
> Will know through this to seek out fear and hate –
> And recognize the realms from which they spring.

Benedictus

> Begin to know yourself in cosmic words –
> And feel yourself in power of cosmic thought.

And as you've now beheld outside yourself
What you in dreaming saw as your own nature,
So find *yourself* – and shudder not, in future,
At the word, which rightfully resounds,
And which shall show to you your own being.

Capesius　　From now on, therefore, I may be my own
Again. And I will seek myself, for seeing
Myself in cosmic thought, I now may live.

Benedictus　Then join all you have won, just now, to what
You've gained before, as something for the world.

In the background, Felicia Balde appears at Benedictus' side, dressed in her ordinary clothes.

Felicia (*in the tone of one telling a fairy-tale*)
Once there was a radiant child of Gods.
It felt itself at one in spirit-worlds
With all those beings who weave in wisdom there.
It grew up, cared for by the father of truth,
To be a primal power within his realm.
And as it felt its ripened will creating,
Stirring, in its radiant body of light,
It often gazed with deep compassion to
The Earth, where souls all longed for truth.
And turning to the father of truth, it said:
"Human beings are thirsting for the drink
Which you can give them, from your heavenly source."
The father of truth, in serious mood, replied:
"The sources over which I must stand guardian
Let light stream out from shining spirit-suns;
And only beings who do not need to thirst
For air to breathe are able to drink light.
And this is why I raised that child, on light,
Who feels compassionate for earthly souls,
And can bring light to birth in those who breathe.

So find your way to human beings and bring
The light within their souls towards my light,
In holy trust and quickened by the spirit."
The radiant being of light then turned to those
Who breathe, and doing so, experience life.
On earth it found good people everywhere
Who welcomed it with joy into their souls.
It guided then their gaze, in faithful love,
Towards the father at the source of light.
And when the being heard the people speak,
With happy minds, about *imagination* –
As though it was a magic word – it knew
It had been joyfully experienced
Within good human hearts. But then, one day –
A man approached who had no feeling for
The being, who gave it cold and distant looks.
"I guide people's souls on earth to the father of truth
At the source of light", the being said to the stranger.
The man replied: "You weave just wild dreams
In people's spirits and deceive their souls."
And since that day, when this was spoken, many
People slander and reject that being,
Who's able to bring light to breathing souls.

The Soul Forces – Philia, Astrid, Luna and the 'Other Philia' – appear in a cloud
of light.

Philia   The human soul finds,
                That drinks of the light,
                In fields high above,
                It strongly awakes.

Astrid   The spirit can feel,
                That lives unafraid,
                Experiencing worlds,
                It forcefully stands.

Luna   The man has the will,
         Who strives for the heights,
         In grounds of his being,
         With strength to endure.

The Other Philia
         Man's efforts aspire
         To the Bearer of light
         Who opens up worlds
         Which quicken in men
         The zest for delight.
         Ecstatic amazement
         Distracting the spirit,
         In bright heavenly fields,
         Awakens in souls
         The radiance of beauty.
         What's won now, can comfort
         The feelings which venture
         To tread upon thresholds
         So strongly protected
         From souls that know fear.
         And strength it is found
         By the ripening will
         Which fearless encounters
         The spirit creators
         Sustainers of worlds.

Curtain – while Benedictus, Capesius, Maria, Felicia, Lucifer, Ahriman and the four Soul Forces are still in their places.

Scene Seven

A landscape of fantastic forms. It is majestically composed – out of forms created by swirling masses of water on one side, and out of blazing, whirling flames on the other side. In the middle, there is a chasm, from which fire flashes out, which towers upwards to a kind of portal, in front of a form, in the shape of a mountain, made of fire and water.

Guardian   What wild, unbridled wishes thunder here?
              Thus rage those souls, who would approach me here
              Before they've won true quietness, within.
              Such be(i)ngs are merely driven by desire –
              Not by that power which when it speaks creates –
              Because it could create itself in silence.
              Such souls as these I must send back to earth.
              In spirit-realms they would spread chaos and
              Confusion, and disrupt the deeds that cosmic
              Powers, in their wisdom, are preparing.
              They'd even do great damage to themselves.
              Their self-begotten wild, destructive urges
              They'll deem exalted forces of creation,
              For they will take delusion to be truth
              When earth's dark veil can give them no protection.

Johannes and Maria appear.

Johannes   You do not see, before you here, the soul
              That in the past so often neared you from
              Johannes, Benedictus's spirit-pupil –
              Although the form Johannes bears on earth
              It still must call its own. That soul approached you,
              Filled with the desire for knowledge. But
              He couldn't bear the nearness of your presence.
              And so, whenever he experienced you,
              He wrapped himself in selfhood. And thus he often
              Gazed on worlds that seemed to show to him

The origin and meaning of existence.
Within those worlds he found the bliss of knowledge –
And the powers, as an artist, which
Could guide his inmost feelings and his hand
Into the very traces of creation –
In such a way that he in truth believed
That cosmic powers experienced themselves
In him, and left the record in his paintings
Of their work. He did not know that nothing
Lived in all he thought as he created
But his own soul. Just like a spider, wrapped
In self-created webs, he merely spun
Himself, and thought himself the world.
He once believed he saw Maria in spirit
But only saw the image she had left
In him, mistaken for her spirit-self.
And when, occasionally, he glimpsed himself
In truth, his wish was to escape himself.
He thought he lived in spirit, but could only
Really find himself within his blood.
He learned to know the power of this blood;
This was reality; all else but image.
Through blood alone he gained true vision; and
It showed him who, in distant days on earth,
Had been his father and beloved sister.
His blood led him to blood-relations; then
He knew how strongly we deceive ourselves
When we desire to vainly climb from matter
To the spirit. Spirit-striving often
Binds us more to matter than a life
That's dimly stumbled through. Realizing this,
Johannes hurled himself into the hands
Of him who even in his seeming could
Not thus deceive; of Lucifer, who's real,
Even just as image. Gods only

Approach mankind in truth; but Lucifer
Remains himself if seen as false or true.
And so I know it's a reality
I feel, believing I must find that soul
Which he did bind to me within his realm.
Possessed of all the power that Lucifer
Can lend, I'll force my way beyond your threshold,
Knowing there I'll find my Theodora.

Guardian   Johannes, be aware of what you know!
What lies beyond this threshold is not known
To you: and yet you know all my demands
Before you can set foot within this realm.
You must first free yourself from many powers
You've gained within your earthly body's life.
You are only permitted to retain
What has been granted you in purest spirit-
Striving, and which has stayed pure.
But this you've thrown away to Ahriman –
And what was left has Lucifer corrupted.
I must take all this from you at the threshold
If you desire to rightly pass across.
Then *nothing* will remain. In spirit-lands
You'll find yourself a being who *has* no being.

Johannes   I *will* have *being* – and will find Theodora –
She must become my source of heavenly light,
That always for her soul beyond the earth
Reveals itself with such abundant grace.
I need no more than this. And *you* in vain
Oppose my path, even if the power I've gained
On earth does not match up to all your past
Opinions of what goodness is in spirit.

Maria   You, who since the origins of Earth,
Have had to guard the threshold to this realm,

You know what is required of beings of
Your age and kind if they're to enter it;
And human beings who encounter you,
If they just bring themselves, and cannot show
Rich fruits of spirit-striving, also must
Be turned away, go back to earthly life.
But to your threshold this one here could bring
The other soul, to whom he's closely linked
By destiny. High spirit-powers have
Appointed you to keep all human beings
Back, who if they passed beyond your threshold
Would but bring destruction on themselves.
Your Portal, though, you are allowed to open
To those souls, who feel that love in spirit-
Realms, and let it permeate their being,
Which your gods had foreordained for them,
Before in battle they were stood against
By Lucifer. Before his throne my heart
Has made the solemn vow to serve such love
Through future times, so knowledge poured into
Men's souls by Lucifer may never harm it.
And people, from now on, will always need
To find each other, who, with strength of mind,
Can listen to the love-filled revelation
Of the gods, as once they listened to
The words that Lucifer could speak of knowledge.
Johannes, when within his earthly body,
Now has little hearing for my voice,
Compared with when in previous days on earth,
I showed to him what in Hibernia's sacred
Places I myself had come to know
About that God who lives in men and once
Did triumph over death itself because
He lived love's very being. My friend will learn,
In spirit-realms, to hear again the Word

From me, for which his ear is dulled on earth,
Deluded as it is by Lucifer.

Johannes (*as if beholding a being in the spirit*)
Maria, do you see – the venerable
Old man, flowing robes – his serious face –
And noble brow – such radiance in his eyes.
He walks through crowded lanes and streets, but all
With reverence let him pass, not wishing to
Disrupt his train of thought, for one can see
With what great power of thinking, deep within
Himself, he contemplates essential truths.
Maria, do you see?

Maria   I see him, yes –
With your soul's eye. To you alone, though,
Does he wish to show himself. This vision
Is of great significance for you.

Johannes   I'm seeing now into his soul. Within
Its depths resounds what he's just heard; before
His eyes there stands his wise, beloved teacher.
Just now he was with him. The teacher's words
Fill up his soul. His thinking moves right to
The fountainhead of all existence;
As people in long-distant days on earth,
Although their souls still lived but as in dream,
Could be so near perceiving worlds of spirit.
The old man's soul is travelling paths of thought
That he has heard from his exalted teacher.
But now he's vanished from my inner gaze.
If I could see him but a little longer.

I now behold, within the crowd, some men
Discussing him. I hear their words. They speak
Of that old man with absolute respect.

In youth he was a bold and mighty warrior,
Burning with ambition and desire
For fame; and desperate to be hailed the greatest
Fighter in his ranks; in battle-service
He committed fierce and numberless
Atrocities, upon his quest for glory.
And often he would cause much blood to flow.
But then there came the time when luck
Upon the battlefield left him. In
Disgrace he journeyed home and there met scorn
And mockery. Full of pride and still in search
Of fame his soul was filled with violent hatred.
He saw his fellow-men as enemies
To be destroyed when opportunity
Allowed. But as he saw that even with
A thousand swords he could not hope to take
Revenge on all his en(e)mies, he began
To overcome himself. He conquered pride
And lust for fame. And in old age he made
The further resolution then to join
The little group of spirit-pupils meeting
In his town. The man, who was the teacher
Of this circle bore within him all
The wisdom Masters from primeval times
Had handed down to the Initiates.
I hear this from those men within the crowd.

My heart expands with warmest love when I
Perceive, in inner sight, this aged man,
Who after all his battles, urged on by
Ambition, won the greatest battle human
Beings can win – he overcame – himself.
But why, here, do I behold this man,
Whose very image blesses me. The feelings

He evokes cannot be new. Through many
Previous lives we must be linked for me
To feel such overwhelming love as this.
I must have been his pupil once and gazed
On him with eyes of wonder. How I long
To meet again, right now, the soul that knew
This body as its own – wherever it
May be – on earth or somewhere else. I'll show
It all the strength of love I feel. This soul
Will bring to life in me again good forces,
That worthy, solemn, human bonds created.

Maria   But are you sure, Johannes, that this soul,
If it approached you now, would still appear
In all its former holiness and light?
What if it's caught in feelings quite unworthy
Of its former state? For many human beings
Would blush with shame if they could see how far
They are from what they once have been. Perhaps
This man is filled with passions, helplessly
Misled by his desires, and you would look
On him in tragic disillusionment
And grief.

Johannes   Maria, how can you say these words?
I don't see what could make make you say this?
Do thoughts move very differently here
Than in the places that we know on earth?

Guardian   What is revealed to you, Johannes, in
This place, brings you a *testing* of your soul.
Now gaze into dark layers of your being.
You wish for this, unknowingly – yet still
May do it. That which has lain hidden from
You, in your depths, as long as you lived blindly,

     Lucifer appears

Will now appear before you, robbing you
Of all the darkness that's protected you.
Now recognize the human soul for whom
You long with burning love – which lived within
The body of the aged man you see.
So recognize who you most strongly love.

Lucifer   Immerse yourself within your being's depths
              And recognize your strongest powers of soul.
              Then learn to know how strength of love alone
              Can raise you up within the worlds of change.

Johannes   Yes, at last I feel the soul who wished
              To show herself to me – yes – Theodora –
              She appeared to me. She wished to stand
              Before me for she knew that I will see
              Her once beyond this threshold. I may love
              Her; I have seen her in a previous life.
              This shows to me my love is right and good.
              In you alone I'll find myself again
              And through you attain my future goal.

Guardian   I have no power to stop what you will do.
              You have seen in image-form that soul
              You love most deeply. You will see it again
              Beyond my threshold. See and feel if it
              Can bring the blessed healing that you dream.

The Other Philia
              O do not heed the solemn Guardian, appearing
              He leads you into barren wastes
              Of life – and takes away all human
              Warmth. His vision scans the spirit-heights,
              But knows not human suffering –
              Which souls can only bear
              When wrapped in warmth of earthly love

Against cold cosmic spaces.
Austerity he knows
But gentleness abhors
And powers of desire
He's hated since
The genesis of earth.

Curtain.

Scene Eight

The realm of Ahriman. A dark ravine-like space, enclosed by mountains, made of black masses of rock, which tower up in fantastic forms. They reveal skeletons everywhere, which appear to crystallize out of the mountain masses, but in white. Ahriman stands on a ledge. Hilary and Friedrich Trautmann enter.

Friedrich Trautmann
> I've visited this kingdom countless times.
> But nonetheless – it seems to me so dreadful
> That, precisely here, we often gain
> Instruction for some task essential for
> Our Brotherhood and for the goals we serve.

Hilary
> The seed that rises greenly from the earth
> Must first have died. Down here, all dead things come –
> But not to rot. For here they are transformed
> And win new life; and if our Brotherhood
> Desires to plant the seeds for future deeds
> Of men, it must draw life from worlds of death.

Trautmann
> The Lord that governs here is sinister;
> And if it was not stated in our books –
> Which are the greatest treasures of our Temple –
> That he we meet here's good – then often one
> Would think that he is evil.

Hilary
>   Not just books.
> My spirit-vision also says to me
> That goodness is what he reveals. You'll see.

Ahriman (*in a disguised voice*)
> I know why both of you are here again.
> Johannes has just wandered from the path;
> You're hoping to discover, in my realm,
> How rightly you may lead that human soul,
> Who often now has stood upon your threshold.

Because you think Johannes wholly lost,
It seems to you that Strader now must be
The man to serve your Mystic Brotherhood.
But he, in fact, has me to thank for what,
From natural forces, he has won for human
Progress; for it's me who is the ruler,
There, where from the sources of creation,
Forces gain their strength, which can be used
Mechanic(a)lly. And so, whatever it
May be he will create for humankind,
Will also have to turn towards my realm.
But, this time, I will take charge myself
Of what from now on happens with the man.
For with Johannes all your work could just
Have brought me grief. And so, if you
Desire to serve the spirit-powers, then
With Strader, you must first attempt to earn
What with Johannes you let slip away.

Ahriman becomes invisible

Trautmann (*after a pause in which he withdraws into himself*)
My noble master, something weighs on me.
I've kept on trying to ignore it, knowing
What's demanded by our Brotherhood;
But much of what takes place within our ranks
Brings a bitter struggle in my soul.
I've always tried to keep my dark thoughts down,
So grateful for the spirit-light you shone;
But often clearly seeing you deceived,
And how your words have proved so gravely wrong,
I've felt as if a nightmare haunted me
That harshly robbed my soul of any peace.
Now yet again your words are clearly false.
You seriously believe the spirit here
Can be in any way a source of good?

Hilary   The cosmic ways are strange and hard to grasp.
               I see, dear brothers, we will have to wait,
               Till higher powers reveal to us the way
               That's in accordance with the work we do.

                    Hilary and Trautmann leave.

Ahriman (*who has reappeared*)
               They see me, but can't recognize me. Fools!
               For if they knew who reigns here, they would never
               Journey here for help. A visitor
               Of mine they'd piously condemn to hell!

*The twelve people enter, who had gathered in the antechamber of the Mystic
Brotherhood at the beginning – though it is indicated that they are walking
blindly in Ahriman's realm. They speak words, which do indeed live in their souls,
but which they know nothing about. They are experiencing unconscious dreams
in their sleep, which can be heard in Ahriman's realm. Strader, however, who
has also entered, is half conscious in relation to what he experiences, and so will
later be able to remember it.*

Strader   Inspired by Benedictus, I have worked
               To grasp the inner power of thinking's life.
               It's led me here – the kingdom of the dead.
               How strange. I'd hoped to rise into the spirit
               And there receive the truth from wisdom's heights.

Ahriman   If you conduct yourself aright, the wisdom
               To be gained here could suffice your soul
               For ages hence.

Strader   And who is this my soul
               Confronts? Which spirit speaks in you?

Ahriman   You'll know him later if you can recall
               What you've experienced here.

Strader   And why are all
               These people drifting through your dark domain?

Ahriman   Their souls alone are in this place, aware
Of nothing; for at home their bodies lie
In deepest sleep. But here will be revealed,
As clear as day, what's in their souls, and what
When they're awake, they rarely know.
They cannot hear a word of what we say.

Louisa Fürchtegott
The soul should not unreasoningly believe
In revelations, striving, sick with pride,
For light-filled, mystic states. I stand with strength
Upon the solid ground of modern science.

Ahriman (*only audible to Strader*)
You cannot guess how drenched with pride you are –
And blindly lead yourself into the dark.
She'll offer you good service, Strader, in
Your work, attained through me; for that she needs
No faith in spirit, which her pride disdains.

Friedrich Geist
The mystic paths are powerfully alluring:
In future I will never lack the zeal
To give myself completely to the wisdom
That I can garner from the Temple's words.

Michael Edelmann
My pure heart hungers for the truth; my prayers
Ascend to heaven. Surely my desire
For light will lift me to the highest realms,
Where I will shine: the temple's best disciple.

Georg Wahrmund
The spirit-treasures of true mysticism,
Whenever they have been revealed to me,
Affect me deeply and they always have;
Wholeheartedly I will contiunue striving.

Ahriman (*only audible to Strader*)

> They mean it well; but all their striving's weak
> And superficial. Thus I can exploit
> Their spirit-essence, using it to serve
> My enterprise for many decades still.
> They too appear quite useful for my goal
> To make your new technology unfold
> With brilliance and amazement for mankind.

Maria Treufels

> When reverence for the universe unites
> With clearest sight of life's realities –
> The healthy sense for life will of itself
> Bring to the soul the ripest spirit-fruits.

Ahriman (*only audible to Strader*)

> She speaks, in dreaming, of realities;
> She'll dream then even better when she wakes.
> And thus I'll have no joy of her for now
> But more, I hope, next time around. For then
> She'll be an occultist and on demand
> Disclose men's former lives since earth began.
> But loyalty's not in her: in a previous life
> She slated you viciously, whilst now
> She highly praises you. Things change, you see.
> For now, she'll bring more luck to Lucifer.

Franzisca Demut

> The lofty realm that mysticism knows
> Will one day form our being as a whole,
> When thoughts receive their nourishment from feelings,
> And feelings let themselves be led by thoughts.

Katherina Ratsam

> Although men strive indeed to find the light
> They do so in a most peculiar way;
> For first they blot it out then are surprised
> That they can never find it in the dark.

Ahriman (*only audible to Strader*)

>These are the souls who love to feel the rightness
>Of their words; but they lack strength beneath.
>For now they're inaccessible to me.
>Their deeds in future, though, will make this change.
>They're miles from what they think themselves to be.

Bernard Redlich

>Imagination is a dangerous friend.
>It tricks the mind with wild, fantastic dreams.
>Be cautious in your quest for knowledge: only
>Strictest thinking masters all life's riddles.

Hermine Hauser

>Creation is a state of ceaseless change.
>All things are fluid, shifting – and evolve –
>Whoever seeks to fix a world in flux
>Will never grasp the mystery of life.

Caspar Stürmer

>The poet and the dreamer waste their days
>In fantasy. Their vigour drains away,
>Enfeebling them for earth-life. What we need
>Is healthy people, helping practically.

Maria Kühne

>A soul that does not mind if it decays
>Will let mere outer forces shape its life.
>The worthy human being wants to grow
>And to develop what she bears within.

Ahriman (*only audible to Strader*)

>What these poor souls contain is merely human.
>Impossible to know what they'll achieve.
>Let Lucifer do what he wants with them.
>He could make them believe that they do nothing
>But unfold the strength of their own souls.
>And so – perhaps – he hasn't lost them yet.

Ferdinand Reinecke

> To comprehend the world it is enough
> To use plain reason and our common sense.
> To find our way in life we should take hold
> Of what is useful and what we enjoy.
> The quest for wisdom is a pointless game –
> That makes great claims for weak and paltry men.
> High goals can lead to nothing on the earth.

Ahriman (*only audible to Strader*)

> The special, carefully picked philosopher!
> He'll be the same again again in his next life.
> With him I merely balance the accounts.
> From twelve I must keep seven for myself
> And give the other five to Lucifer.
> Sometimes, you see, I look at men and ask
> What kind they are and what each one can do;
> And once I've picked out twelve, my search is done.
> A thirteenth one would be just like the first.
> For then, you see, when I have drawn these twelve
> Into my realm, according to the colour
> Of their souls, then many more must follow.

To himself; so that Strader cannot hear him, he closes Strader's ears.

> In fact I've managed none of this as yet –
> The earth has never wished to yield to me.
> But I will strive through all eternity –
> And make good use of everything I can –
> Till victory one day – perhaps – is mine.

Audibly to Strader again

> You see I do not trade in pretty words
> Nor seek to please mankind. Whoever seeks
> More polished words, as inspiration
> For their goals, must find them somewhere else.

Yet if with reason and a sense for truth
You can observe what happens here, through me,
You'll recognize that only I can give
What's needed, if the children of mankind
Are not to be completely lost on earth.
I'm needed even by the gods; for they
Will only ever free a soul from me
When I have first been active in their depths.
Should one day then my enemies succeed
In making men believe the lie that I
Can ever be dispensed with, souls will dream
Of higher worlds, while power ebbs away.

Strader   You see in me a soul who well might follow
You – and do you service. What I've seen
Here seems to show that only lack of sense
And judgement makes a man your enemy.
No. You used no pretty words. You all
But mocked these souls, as you described their diff(e)rent
Destinies.

What you can offer men,
I must confess, I see as good. Through you
They'll gain the strength for good – and what is evil
This will be their own. And even all
Your mockery, if men would better know
Themselves, they'd share with all their heart.

But what strange pow(e)r compels my soul to speak?
I utter words, which if I found them true
On earth, would shatter and destroy me.

You have to think the way you do, and I
Can do no other than accept your words.
But only here is it the truth; if it

Should try and prove itself on earth, it would
Be false. I can't go on with normal powers
Of thinking......They are blocked...... Are at an end.

What's this? In all the roughness of your words
There echoes out – your pain. And suffering.
Hearing it, I too am filled with pain.

To see you – makes me just – lament and weep.

Strader exits quickly.

Maria and Johannes appear, both fully conscious – so that they can hear all that happens and can speak consciously.

Johannes	Maria, this place is filled with terror. Fear Is dense and presses right into my being. Where can I find the strength to ward it off?
Maria	My solemn, holy vow rays out its strength; Allow yourself to feel its healing power – If you're to bear the pressure of this place.
Ahriman (*to himself*)	Ha! These two are sent by Benedictus So they can gain experience of me here And thus may come to know me.

The rest is spoken so that Johannes and Maria can hear it.

The Guardian, Johannes, had to send
You here, into my realm, upon your way
Towards that light you seek in depths of being.
I can give you truth – and bitter pain –
That pain I've suffered for millennia –
For though the truth can reach me here, it must
First wholly separate itself from joy –
Before it dares to enter through my gates.

Johannes   Bereft of joy, then, let me see that soul
            Whom I desire so burningly to see.

Ahriman   All wishes and desires need warmth of soul;
            But here – all wishes freeze – in ice and cold.

Maria   And in the endless, empty fields of ice,
            I've gained the right to lead my friend, where he
            Will win that light, which spirits must create,
            When darknesses can lame the powers of life.
            Now feel, Johannes, all your strength of soul.

                The Guardian appears on the threshold

Ahriman   The Guardian himself must bring that light
            For which your soul so passionately yearns.

Johannes   I will behold her clearly – Theodora!

The Guardian
            The soul that you did see upon my threshold,
            Appearing as it lived in former times,
            Enflamed in you, at this your time of trial,
            The strongest powers of love within your soul.
            As you still stood outside this realm, and sought
            To pass across, you saw his soul as image.
            But images that spring from wishes often
            Mask illusion. Now, though, see in truth
            The soul that lived within that aged man.

Johannes   I see him once again, in flowing robes –
            That warrior in youth, who in old age
            Could conquer his own self. O noble soul,
            Who graced this form, why have you hid yourself
            From me so long. I know you well. I know
            You must be Theodora. Noone else.
            Your veiled image changes – shows you as
            You really are – yes! Theo…. I *myself.*

At the syllables 'Theo', the Double appears.

The Double (*coming right up to Johannes*)
      Recognize me. See in me *yourself*.

Maria   And I may follow *you* to depths of worlds,
      Where souls attain the feeling of the gods,
      Through shatt(e)ring inner victories that destroy,
      And boldly from destruction win back being.

Thunder and gathering darkness.

Curtain.

Scene Nine

A friendly landscape in morning sunlight. There is a town in the background, with many factory buildings. Benedictus, Capesius, Maria, Johannes and Strader walk freely back and forth in conversation, in different groupings.

Capesius   It is here, in gentle morning sunlight,
     Where Benedictus often turns himself
     Devotedly towards his pupils, who,
     In hallowed mood, can listen to his wisdom.
     Over there, lies all that cuts off souls
     So ruthlessly from all the wondrous beauty
     That surrounds us here, where we receive
     Such blessing from the holiness in nature.
     Amidst the desolation of that sea
     Of houses, Benedictus constantly
     Endeavours, through his loving deeds, to heal
     And lessen people's bitter suffering.
     But when he wisely tells his pupils of
     The spirit-worlds, in words they understand,
     He wishes then for hearts that have been opened,
     Sun-like, through the free pow(e)rs of creation,
     That here reveal themselves, awaking souls.
     I, too, am by good fortune now permitted
     To gain the blessing that his words can give.
     He's taken on the burden, lovingly,
     Of guiding me, in spirit, into spirit
     Realms. And so, whenever he is near,
     I feel as if I am myself again.

Benedictus (*approaching*)
     A knot, Capesius, woven from the threads
     Of karma, in the circle of my pupils,
     At last begins to loosen. Your free deeds
     And those of others lead to this unravelling.

Find your helpers now – in hearts devoted
To the spirit-guidance I too serve.
United with them you'll complete the work
For which you have been well-prepared in spirit.

Capesius   I've recognized you and will follow you.
I gazed into my soul, after I'd heard
Your words, like be(i)ngs, in spirit-worlds, and you'd
Restored me to myself; and then I saw,
In spirit-light, the goals which all my future
Lives on earth must serve. And now I know
It is from you I'll find my proper way.

Benedictus   If you unite with Strader and Johannes
You can do much to bring about a healing
In mankind. Your different powers of soul
Have been prepared through many lives, so that
Together you may form a trinity,
Which will be able to do much on earth.

Capesius   Then I must thank the strict unbending powers
Of destiny – which I had found so cruel
And meaningless at first – for showing me,
When it was right, my purposes in life.

A pause while he considers

How wonderfully you led me. First it seemed
Impossible to lift myself into
Those worlds of spirit that your words portrayed.
For ages, when I sank into your works,
I just met thoughts; then all at once I found
Myself within the very life of spirit-
Worlds. I barely knew then how to live
And be within the ordinary world.

Benedictus   The ordinary, outer world would always
Have concealed for you the life of spirit;

Had this not dampened down this outer world,
Through stronger power, and rendered it a shadow.
Thus you have had to know full spirit-sight,
While others first must open eyes of soul.

*During Capesius's last words, Strader approaches; the three of them walk away,
and after a short time, Benedictus returns with Strader.*

Strader   Your words transported me beyond my Earthly form.
             Awaking to myself once more,
             Within my body, I was filled with deep
             And numbing pain. The sorrow that I felt
             In time brought back the memory of all
             I'd been through, up until that terrifying
             Moment when, in front of Ahriman,
             I had to see how there all thinking stops.
             And then I had to question – why your words
             Should lead me to that place where souls are only
             Seen as units fitted to what he
             Desires to make out of my work. He picks
             Out twelve and seeks to make them serve his ends.

Benedictus   You know, though, why those souls that Ahriman
             Displayed to you, precisely sought your help,
             When he desired to influence their fate?

Strader   All this was also shown me by my pain.
             I saw what in a previous life had linked me
             To those within the spiritual Brotherhood.
             Its members reappear today as those
             Who lead the Mystic Temple. And I saw
             As well how in the mediaeval days
             The peasants treated me, who now are these
             Twelve citizens. I felt how Ahriman
             Is wishing to exploit the bond that must
             Still keep them tied to me in future lives.

Benedictus   The cosmic powers always guide their deeds
              According to right measurement and number,
              So that they're wisely woven in the world.
              The outer senses see the sun pursue
              Its path through twelve stellar constellations.
              This shows how through long ages things unfold
              On earth. These powers will shine into your work.
              But Ahriman desired to use those powers,
              Instead, to shape those human souls themselves,
              And bind them to you by strict laws of number.

Strader   As I have grasped both measurement and number
              I'll know in future how to free my work
              From Ahriman's domain, and make it be
              Of rightful service to the gods of earth.

Benedictus   You have had to learn through Ahriman
              The universal sense of numbers' laws;
              This was necessary for *your* soul.
              You had to know this realm, according to
              Your path into the spirit, for your true
              Creative gifts to blossom and bear fruit.

They exit. Maria and Johannes enter from other side.

Maria   Johannes, happily you have succeeded
              In winning knowledge from cold realms of truth.
              No longer will you weave in images
              What souls within the body only dream.
              For thoughts that would spring only from themselves
              Are very far indeed from world-becoming.

Johannes   And that they do this, happens from self-love
              Which likes to see itself as thirst for knowledge.

Maria   Whoever wishes to devote himself
              To human progress, and to perform deeds
              Of living power, within the course of time,

Must first entrust himself to powers, who through
Their battling, are able to bring measure
And number, both in order and in chaos,
Into deep world realities. For only then
Does knowledge first become true life,
That can reveal itself in human souls,
When they can bring to memory in the body
What they've experienced in spirit-realms.

Johannes   I see my path. I have to feel myself
As twofold from now on. Through you and
Benedictus, I'm a being that knows itself
In spirit, who possesses faculties
That aren't my own. What you've both given is
Another man within me – ready now
To give to others what he has been graced
With. He will serve the world as best he can,
But nothing from my normal self must mingle
With it, marring this new man, who knows
That he's but at the start of true self-knowledge.
He'll guide his own steps forward, helped by you,
And thus will form his destiny in future.

Maria   Whether you walk in paths of truth or error,
You'll always hold the doorway open,
Through which your soul may take its rightful steps,
If you can learn to bear courageously
Necessities that spring from spirit-realms.

Curtain.

Scene Ten

The temple of the Mystic Brotherhood which appeared in Scenes One and Two.
At the beginning of the scene Benedictus and Hilary stand in the East; Bellicosus
and Torquatus in the South; Trautmann in the West.

Benedictus   My pupils have each found the way, according
           To their different paths of destiny,
           To let the spirit-light shine in their souls.
           What each one has achieved must now bear fruit
           For both the others. This can only happen
           If they are willing, in this sacred place,
           To join their strengths, in true and rightful measure,
           To form a higher unity. Through this
           They'll waken, for the first time, to true life
           What must, if they're apart, remain as being.
           They stand upon the threshold of this temple
           Of initiation. May they now
           Unite their souls and let them sound together,
           As world-destiny decrees – so that
           The harmony of spirits can attain
           What one alone cannot. To what has
           Worthily held sway here since the dawn of time
           They will bring something new. The pupils I
           Will lead before you, you my temple-brothers,
           Have had to face harsh trials in spirit-worlds
           To find their way here. They'll respect the sacred
           Rites and ancient holy practices
           Which here shine out their spirit-light. Yourselves,
           Who've faithfully performed, for many years,
           This spirit-service, will receive new tasks
           In future. Only for a time does cosmic
           Destiny call men to serve within
           The Temple. Then it gives them other tasks.
           The temple has itself been sorely tested.

Guardian of the light, it was protected
From darkness, in a grave and fateful hour,
By the error of one man. Johannes
Recognized, unconsciously, he should
Not cross the threshold to this temple till
He'd crossed that other threshold, of which this
One's but a symbol. So he closed the doors
Upon himself, which you had wished, through love,
To open to him. Now he'll reappear
To you, another man and worthily
Receive from you initiation's blessing.

Hilary   We humbly seek to offer to the spirit
What ripens and bears fruit within our souls.
And wish to strive so that our wills become
The revelation of the spirit's will.
The temple's led, unfailingly, by wisdom's
Powers – you show the path that you could read
Within the cosmic book of destiny
When each of these your pupils passed their trials.
So let them enter and unite their strength
With ours, here in this hallowed sanctuary.

*At a knock from Hilary – Johannes, Capesius, Maria, Felix Balde, Felicia Balde
and Strader enter the Temple. Trautmann and Torquatus lead in those entering,
in such a way that Johannes stands in front of Benedictus and Hilary; Capesius
in front of Bellicosus and Torquatus; Strader in front of Trautmann; and Maria
stands with Felix and Felicia in the middle of the Temple.*

Hilary   My son, the words one utters in this place,
Incur a crying guilt in spirit-worlds,
Unless they are inspired by truth alone.
And just as great as is this guilt are all
The forces of destruction it unleashes
Upon the one unworthy to be here.
Aware of the effect of temple words,

The man who stands before you has attempted
To serve, as best he can, the spirit-world,
Before the holy symbol of that Light
Which shines from out the East upon our Earth.
It is the will of destiny that you
Become the one to serve now at this altar.
But know this too: the one who gives you this
Authority, and these the keys of his
High office, gives you also all his blessing –
With all the power that this place imparts.

Johannes   Exalted Master! Only folly and
Presumption, in the frail human being
Before you here, could ever make him wish
That he might now succeed you in your holy work.
He does not have the right to take a single step
Across the threshold of this Temple. Yet
What he could never wish upon himself,
Must humbly be accepted when he's called
By powers of destiny. I had to know
Myself, in spirit-realms, completely worthless.
It was not I, therefore, who could allow
Myself to stand here. Benedictus, though,
And my true friend, Maria, have formed in me,
A second man; of which my former self,
In time, will merely be the bearer. Yes –
I have been granted, on my path of spirit,
A self, which can be strong, and can reveal
Its full, creative powers, even if
The bearer still must know himself far distant
From the highest human goals. When thus
We feel the second man awake in us,
We always have to keep this stringent rule
Before our spirit-eye: that nothing from
Our personal self may ever be allowed

To enter, jarringly, into that work
Not done by us but by our second self.
Within our selves, invisibly, we have
To work, so that we grow, and thus become
What we may be. Our pers(o)nal struggles we
Must bear through life, shut tight within our souls.
That in my personal self I have no right
To stand within this place, I told you when
I first was here. That other self, though, now
Entrusted to me, sees himself as called
By destiny to carry out, as best
He can, the work of guard(i)an from this place,
As long as this is asked him by the Spirit.

Torquatus (*to Capesius*)

Capesius, from now on, at this place,
Where love should stream through wisdom, as the Sun
Streams out its warmth so powerfully at noon,
You shall perform the Temple's sacred service.
Whoever offers up their spirit here,
To serve the mystic work, must face great dangers.
For Lucifer is always able to
Approach, unseen, he who does good service
Here, and to impress on each one of his words
The seal of the opponent of the gods.
You stood before the Adversary's throne,
And could behold what follows from his deeds,
And thus, for your task here, are well prepared.

Capesius

When one has seen the Adversary's realm,
As destiny has granted me to do,
One knows that good and evil are but words
That people hardly ever understand.
Whoever would see Lucifer as only
Evil, should say that fire too is evil,
Because it has the power to destroy,

ipis

And should call water evil too, because
In it someone may drown.

Torquatus	Lucifer

Appears evil, then, through other things
And not through what he signifies himself.

Capesius   That cosmic spirit who, when earth began,
Was able to bring light to human souls,
Must perform tasks within the universe
Which, to spirits who can understand
Necessities, prove neither good nor evil.
For good can turn to evil, if a bad
Intention, serving but itself, corrupts it;
And what seems evil can transform to good
If beings of goodness guide it on its path.

Torquatus   And thus you know what you will always need
When standing here. For Love, it does not judge
The powers at work within the universe.
It values them, and asks how it may use
Whatever springs to life from grounds of worlds.

Benedictus   But Love will often speak in quiet words
And needs to be supported in the soul.
It therefore will unite itself to all
That wills to serve, in noble trinity,
The spirit-goals belonging to the Temple.
Maria will unite her work with yours.
The vow she spoke in Lucifer's domain
Will radiate its blessing power here.

Maria   The deep words you, Capesius, have spoken,
Are true, when rightly springing from that spirit
Who shows to human beings the way of Love;
But lead to error upon error when
They spring from bad intentions and transform

To evil in men's souls. There is no doubt
That Lucifer reveals himself before
Our souls, as Bearer of the Light, when these
Turn to the spirit-realm. The human soul,
Though, always wishes to awaken in
Itself, what it should only gaze upon,
With wonder. Souls should see the radiant beauty
Lucifer reveals, but never fall
Under its power, so he can work within them.
When he, the bringer of the light streams out
His wisdom, filling words with pride of selfhood,
The bold and free example to all beings
Of shining individuality –
Then may the soul rejoice in bringing out
Its inwardness, and celebrate in joy
All it can feel and all it loves in life.
But human beings, more than other spirits,
Need that God, who does not only claim
Our wonder, as he shines in outer glory –
Who only then reveals his greatest power
When he takes up his dwelling in the soul
And who proclaims with love the life in death.
The human being can turn to Lucifer
To feel delight in all that shines as beauty;
Through this he may well feel himself; but must
Not wish that Lucifer be his own being.
But to that other spirit humans call
When they have rightly learned to know themselves:
It is the loving goal of earth's own soul:
Not I, but Christ is living in my being.

Benedictus (*turning to Maria*)

Your soul, Mari(a), when it turns to the spirit,
As it vowed to do, before the throne
Of Lucifer, is strong enough to shine

Into this Temple, showing it the ways
Of healing for the world; and Christ will shine
With warmth and light, the sense of spirit-love
Within this place. What your soul thus can offer
To the world is linked to your own life
By one partic(u)lar knot of destiny.
Once long ago a son turned from his father
Due to you. And now you lead the son
Back to the father. In a former life
Johannes was Capesius's son.
The father asks no longer that Maria
Repays her debt to him through Lucifer –
For now she has erased her debt through Christ.

Bellicosus (*speaking to Hilary and Benedictus – often turning to Felix and
Felicia*)

Light from spirit-heights is streaming now
With power into the sanctuaries – if souls
Can rightly open to it. But those high
And lofty powers of wisdom which reveal
Themselves in temples such as this one now
Have also chosen other paths to souls.
The signs of these our present times show clearly
That all these different paths must now unite.
The Temple has to link with souls who have
Not sought the light along its paths
And yet are also inwardly illumined.
In Felix and Felicia there step
Such souls into this holy sanctuary
Who bring to it their rich, abundant light.

Felicia   All I can do is tell those fairy tales,
Whose images arise, completely by
Themselves in me – about the source of these
In spirit all I know is what Capesius
Would often say. I humbly must believe

All I would hear, when he described by soul's
True character; and thus I also accept
What you describe of why the Temple's called me.

Felix   I've come not just because you summoned me.
I am obedient to the spirit-core
Of my own being; and it guided me,
Entirely independently, to seek
This temple-sanctuary. Many times, my soul
Has journeyed in the higher worlds. At first,
A crushing loneliness approaches you;
All littleness is stripped away, leaving
Only your spirit core, which must be strong
And patient to endure. Eventually,
The darkness dwindles and you find yourself,
At one with everything and full of light.
I found myself within that world which showed
To me the deepest grounds of our existence.
Upon such spirit-pilgrimage I've often
Found my way to living temples just
As like to this one here, that we can see,
As living spoken words are like our writing.

Trautmann (*to Strader*)
Your task, dear Strader, is to speak that word
In future, in the Temple, which, compared
To what Johannes speaks will be as sunset
To the hopeful glow of dawn. You had
To stand in spirit at that place which brings
All thinking to a standstill. As your hand
Could only strike a hammer in the air,
And never feel its strength, without an anvil,
So could thinking never realise
Itself, if Ahriman did not oppose it.
Within your life, your thinking always led
To obstacles, which caused you pain and bitter

Doubt. Through these you learned to know yourself
In thinking, as the light can only see
Its radiant power through reflection. Life's
Reflection is revealed in image, by
The Temple servant's word that's spoken here.

Strader   For long, it's true, the light of thought shone only
As reflection in my life. But then
For seven years the spirit showed itself
To me in brightest light, and opened up
My soul to worlds, before which, previously
My thinking had stood still, in pain and doubt.
This light, now made more inward in my soul,
Will never die throughout eternity,
If I can realize my spirit-goals,
And if there should spring healing from my work.

Theodora (*becoming visible as a spiritual being at Strader's side*)
I have been able to win light for you,
Because your strength aspired to my light,
When finally your time could be fulfilled.

Strader   And thus your light will also shine, you spirit-
Messenger, on all the words my soul
Will speak here. Theodora's being
Is consecrated with me at this place
To carry out this holy task of service.

Philia, Astrid, Luna and the 'Other Philia' appear in a luminous cloud of light.

The Other Philia
From altars of temples
Men's thoughts are arising
To sources of worlds.
What lives in the soul
What strives in the spirit
Wings its way from the world

That is bounded in forms –
And spirits of the worlds incline
In grace towards the souls of men
To kindle spirit light.

Philia   I will beseech from cosmic spirits
That by their beings' light
Be guarded sense for soul,
And that their sounding words
May free the spirit ear
That there may not be lost
What has been wakened
On paths of soul
In human life.

Astrid   I will direct
The streams of love
Which warm the world
Into the spirits
Of the initiates;
That in the hearts of men
The hallowed mood
May be preserved.

Luna   From the primeval powers
I'll beg for strength and courage
And make these the helpers
Of willing sacrifice;
That it may change
What times behold
To spirit seeds
That grow throughout eternities.

*Curtain while all, including Theodora, Philia, Astrid, Luna and
the 'Other Philia', are still in the Temple.*

Rudolf Steiner's Fourth Mystery Drama

The Souls Awaken

Characters, Figures and Events

The spiritual and soul events presented in *The Souls Awaken* should be thought of as taking place about a year after those depicted in the previous Mystery Drama, *The Guardian of the Threshold*.

In *The Souls Awaken* there appear the following characters and beings:

I   **The Bearers of the Spiritual Element:**
     Benedictus. The personality seen by a number of his "pupils" as being the knower of profound spiritual relationships. (He is presented in the previous soul-portrayals, *The Portal of Initiation* and *The Trial of the Soul*, as the leader of the "Sun Temple". In *The Guardian of the Threshold* that spiritual stream comes to expression through him which wishes to put a living and present spiritual life in the place of a merely traditional one, such as is preserved by the "Mystic Brotherhood".) In *The Souls Awaken* Benedictus is no longer to be thought of as simply standing above his pupils, but is interwoven, with his own soul-destiny, into the soul-experiences of his pupils.
     Hilary Gottgetreu. The knower of traditional spiritual life, which in his case is linked with his own spiritual experiences. (The same individuality presented in the previous soul-portrayal *The Trial of the Soul* as the Grand Master of a "Mystic Brotherhood".)
     Hilary's Office Manager.
     Hilary's Secretary. (The same personality who appears in The Guardian of the Threshold as Friedrich Geist.)

II   **The Bearers of the Element Of Devotion:**
     Magnus Bellicosus. (Named Germanus in *The Portal of Initiation*. The preceptor of a "Mystic Brotherhood" in *The Trial of the Soul* and *The Guardian of the Threshold*).
     Albert Torquatus. (Named Theodosius in *The Portal of Initiation*. The same individuality appears in *The Trial of the Soul* as the first Master of Ceremonies in the "Mystic Brotherhood" depicted there.)
     Professor Capesius. In *The Trial of the Soul* his individuality appears as the first Preceptor.

Felix Balde. (The bearer in *The Portal of Initiation* of a certain nature mysticism; the bearer here in *The Souls Awaken* of subjective mysticism. The individuality of Felix Balde appears as Joseph Kean in *The Trial of the Soul*.)

III **The Bearers of the Element Of Will:**

Romanus. (He is reintroduced here under the name used for him in *The Portal of Initiation*, because this corresponds with the essence of his being which he has worked through to in the years between *The Portal of Initiation* and *The Souls Awaken*. The name is used for him in *The Guardian of the Threshold* which is to be thought of as his name in the outer world. He is referred to there by that name because his inner life is of only little significance in the events that occur. His individuality appears in *The Trial of the Soul* as the second Master of Ceremonies in the medieval "Mystic Brotherhood".)

Dr. Strader. (His individuality appears in *The Trial of the Soul* as "Simon the Jew".)

Dr. Strader's Nurse. (The same personality who is named Maria Treufels in *The Guardian of the Threshold*. In *The Portal of Initiation* she is called "The Other Maria" because Johannes Thomasius's imaginative knowing forms the imagination of certain powers of Nature in her image. Her individuality appears in *The Trial of the Soul* as the Keans' daughter "Bertha".)

Felicia Balde. (Her individuality appears in *The Trial of the Soul* as "Mrs. Kean".)

IV **The Bearers of the Element Of Soul:**

Maria. (Her individuality appears in *The Trial of the Soul* as "The Monk".)

Johannes Thomasius. (His individuality appears in *The Trial of the Soul* as "Thomas".)

Hilary Gottgetreu's Wife.

V   Beings from the Spiritual World:
      Lucifer.
      Ahriman.
      Gnomes.
      Sylphs.

VI   Beings of the Human Spiritual Element:
      Philia, Astrid and **Luna**. The spiritual beings who mediate the connec-
      tion of human soul-forces with the cosmos.
      The Other Philia. The bearer of the element of love, in the world to
      which the spiritual personality belongs.
      The Soul of Theodora. (Her individuality appears in *The Trial of the
      Soul* as Celia, the Keans' foster-daughter of and the sister of "Thomas"
      [in whom the individuality of Johannes Thomasius is presented.])
      The Guardian of the Threshold.
      Johannes Thomasius's Double.
      The Spirit of Johannes's Youth.
      The Soul of Ferdinand Reinecke – in Ahriman's realm in Scene 12.
      (He only appears as Ferdinand Reinecke in *The Guardian of the
      Threshold.*)

VII   The personalities of Benedictus and Maria also appear as thought-expe-
      riences – in the 2nd scene as those of Johannes Thomasius; in the third
      scene as those of Strader. In the 10th scene Maria appears as the
      thought-experience of Johannes Thomasius.

VIII In the 5th and 6th scenes of *The Souls Awaken* the individualities of
      Benedictus, Hilary Gottgetreu, Magnus Bellicosus, Albert Torquatus,
      Strader, Capesius, Felix Balde, Felicia Balde, Romanus, Maria, Johannes
      Thomasius and Theodora appear in the spirit-realm as "souls" – and in
      the temple (in the 7th and 8th scenes of *The Souls Awaken*) as personal-
      ities living in a long-distant past.

With regard to *The Souls Awaken*, a remark may also be made similar to what
has been said about the previous soul-portrayals. Neither the spiritual and
soul events nor the spiritual beings are intended merely symbolically or allegorically. To anyone who wished to interpret them in this way, the true

character and beingness of the spiritual world would remain far distant. Even in the appearance of the thought-experiences (in the 2nd, 3rd and 10th scenes) nothing merely symbolical is presented, but real soul-experiences, which for the person entering the spiritual world are just as real as the people and events of the sense-world. For such a person *The Souls Awaken* presents a completely realistic soul-portrayal. If it was a question of symbolism or allegory I would quite definitely have omitted these portrayals.

In response to many questions I began attempting once again to add some "supplementary remarks" by way of explanation of this "soul-portrayal". As before, however, this time too I have stopped myself making this attempt. It goes against the grain to add something like that to the portrayal which should speak for itself. Both in the conception and the execution of the portrayal such abstractions cannot play any role at all. They would only have a disturbing effect. The spiritual reality that is depicted places itself before the soul with the same necessity as do the things we perceive physically. It is self-evident that the images of spiritual perception seen by healthy spirit-vision relate differently to the beings and events involved than the way perceptions of the physical world relate to their corresponding beings and events. On the other hand it has to be said that the way in which the spiritual events present themselves before the soul perceiving them contains within it, already, both the disposition and the composition of such a portrayal.

R. St.

Munich, August 1913

Scene I

Hilary Gottgetreu's accounting office ("Comptoir"), not very modern in style.
It can be imagined that Hilary is the owner of a factory creating many different
products out of wood.
The Secretary and the Manager are in conversation; (Hilary; later Strader.)

Secretary   And look! Now even our friends in Georgeholme
             Are saying how dissatisfied they are.

Manager   Them as well? The whole thing's really pitiful.
             And always it's the same reasons.
             One also sees how painful these friends find it
             That now they need to break with Hilary.

Secretary   Yes. It's in letter after letter.
             'Lacking in punctuality ...'
             'Workmanship not up to the standards of your competitors
                 in the field ...'
             And wherever I go
             I hear the same thing
             Over and over again.
             The good name and solid reputation of the firm,
             Handed down to us through generations of Hilary's family,
             That once we too were able to increase,
             Is swiftly vanishing.
             The opinion is going round
             That Hilary is being duped
             By so-called visionaries and dreamers
             And that his wild, enthusiastic raptures
             Have robbed him of that conscientiousness and care for detail
             Which before, made all the products of the firm
             Unique and widely known throughout the world.
             The same vast numbers of people
             As used to praise our work so highly
             Are now loudly complaining about it.

Manager   It's been remarked on for a long time already
             How Hilary allows himself to be led into error
             By people seeking for "very special" spiritual powers.
             His soul has always had such inclinations;
             But previously he always knew how to keep them separate
             From the working day.

                 Hilary comes into the room.

Manager (*to the secretary*)
             It's necessary, I think,
             For me to talk with the Head of the Factory alone
             For a little while.

                 The Secretary leaves the room.

             My deep concern and worry
             Make me wish to take the opportunity
             For a rather serious word with you.

Hilary   What is it
             That causes my adviser
             Such concern?

Manager   A whole number of things make it quite clear
             That our production is continuing to decline.
             We are failing to achieve what we should.
             And the voices of complaint are growing louder.
             People say the quality of our products is deteriorating
             And that our competitors are outdoing us.
             Many deplore – quite rightly in my opinion –
             The breakdown of our punctuality,
             Which was once the hallmark of our firm.
             If this continues, even the best friends we have
             Will soon cease to be satisfied with us.

Hilary   I have been fully aware of this for some time.
             To tell you the truth, it doesn't worry me.

I must, of course, though, discuss it with you.
You've been far more than an employee –
You've always stood by me as a loyal friend.
So I'll explain quite clearly
What I've often just hinted at.
Whoever wants to create the new,
Must be able to experience, quite calmly, the collapse of the old.
I have no wish to manage the work in future
The way it's been done up till now.
Making profits, benefiting only a few,
And thoughtlessly generating products for the market of
    earthly life,
With no concern for the consequences,
Seems to me unworthy, since I've understood
How work itself can be ennobled
If it receives the stamp of people active in the spirit.
From now on, Johannes Thomasius, as an artist,
Will lead the new department of our work
That I will build for him nearby.
His spirit will give an artistic form
To what we produce mechanically,
Creating products for everyday use
Which as well as being useful, also have nobility and beauty.
Industry and Art must be united –
Daily life be filled with an aesthetic sense.
Thus, to this corpse-like body –
As I see our work now –
I shall bring the soul –
Which alone can give it meaning.

Manager (*after some reflection*)
    The plan for such a wondrous enterprise
    Goes quite against the spirit of our times.
    For everything that we achieve
    Can only hope to reach perfection

By being very strictly specialized.
The mighty powers in life that utterly impersonally
Combine the different parts to form a whole,
They thoughtlessly give every separate part
A value, which wisdom cannot give it.
And even without this,
Your project would still be in vain.
How would you ever find someone
Capable of carrying out this plan
That you've thought out so beautifully?
I simply don't believe it's possible.

Hilary   My friend, you know I do not follow dreams.
I would never have set myself such high goals,
If a lucky star had not led to me
The man who can bring about what I'm striving for.
It amazes me you haven't noticed
That the man for this is Strader.
One who knows his spirit in its true being,
And has a sense for the highest human tasks
Should not be called a dreamer
If he feels as one such task
The need to provide for this man a field of work.

Manager (*surprised*)
     Strader!
Is he not a living example of how human thinking can
     become blinded
When it loses its grasp of reality?
That his machine originated in genuine spiritual inspiration –
I do not doubt.
And if one day it can be realized,
The healing effects will certainly flow from it
Which Strader believed so close at hand.
But for a long time it will remain only a model,
Because the forces which he needs to make it work

Have not yet been discovered.
It saddens me that you could think
That any good would ever come from entrusting your work
    to this man,
Who has already experienced the shipwreck
Of his boldly thought out creation.
There is no doubt this led him to the spirit-heights,
Which will always lure the human soul,
But souls should not attempt to scale them
Till they've attained the necessary powers.

Hilary   The fact that you've praised the spirit of this man,
While attempting to denounce him,
Only confirms his worth.
According to your own words, it was not his fault
That his invention didn't succeed.
Surely, therefore, to be working among us here,
Where nothing from the outside now opposes him,
Is the right place for him to be.

Manager   Even if I try and overcome all my objections,
And try and think as you do,
There's more that forces me to disagree.
For who will there be to appreciate what you produce,
And show sufficient understanding to make use of it?
All your capital will be swallowed up
Before the work's even begun.
And that will be the end of it.

Hilary   It's completely clear that my plans
Would have to be seen as imperfect
If understanding cannot first be created
For our new approach and new way of working.
What Strader and Johannes are working on
Will need to be brought to completion
At the place which I will set up

For the furthering of spiritual knowledge.
What Benedictus, Capesius and Maria will make known there,
Will awaken in people the need
To permeate daily life with spiritual revelation.

Manager   Well, you'll certainly make your little clique happy
Living just for itself, far from the world.
But you're shutting yourself off from true human life.
I know your aim is to overcome egoism,
But the truth is you'll be feeding it.

Hilary   You seem to think of me as some dreamer
Who thoughtlessly denies the experience life has brought him.
This is exactly what I would be doing,
If for a single moment I saw success the way you do.
What seems valuable to me, may well fail outwardly.
But even if the whole world would ridicule it,
And for this reason it collapses,
Still, it would have been placed here,
On earth, as an example, even if only once.
It will work on, spiritually,
Even if it doesn't survive in earthly life.
A portion of that power will be created in it
Which will eventually bring about
The marriage of spiritual goals and earthly deeds.
Spiritual science makes this clear.

Manager   I had wanted to approach you
With what I felt duty-bound to discuss as an employee of
     your firm.
But the way you speak enables me
Also to speak quite openly with you,
As friend to friend.
Working alongside you, as I have, I've felt the need
For years now, to try and gain knowledge
Of those things you devote yourself to,

And to which you give so much of your energy.
I could learn about this in books
Which sought to reveal spiritual knowledge.
Although the worlds they pointed me towards are closed to me
I was able to imagine for myself, intuitively,
How those human beings must feel
Who devote themselves faithfully to such spiritual disciplines.
Through my own research, I confirmed
What many experts in this field clearly describe
About the type of person who feels at home in the spiritual
    world.
Above all else it struck me
That, in spite of all precautions,
When such people have to leave the high realms of their
    spiritual experience
And return to earth,
They're not able to distinguish between reality and illusion.
Out of the spiritual world in which they have been living,
Certain images emerge
That prevent them correctly perceiving the physical world
And deceptively confuse the power of judgement needed for
    our earthly life.

Hilary   What you put forward as an objection
Merely strengthens me, because it shows
That in you I have one more colleague,
Close to my future plans.
How could I have guessed
That you'd have made yourself familiar
With the kind of souls
Wishing to join me in my work.
You know the dangers which threaten them:
You'll therefore also be able to see from their deeds
That they know the paths which will protect them.
Soon you'll gain a trust in the whole situation;

And in the future I'll find in you,
Yet again, the adviser I cannot do without.

Manager

I cannot give myself to deeds
Whose effects are unclear to me.
The people in whom you put your trust
Seem to me to have fallen into exactly
The kind of delusion of which I spoke.
And those who choose to listen to them
Will be drawn into it as well. Such power of delusion
Overrides all conscious goal-oriented thinking.
You will always find me at your side,
Ready and willing to offer my advice,
For as long as you base your work
On the firm foundation of earthly reality.
Your new way of working, though, is *not for me!*

Hilary

By your refusal, you jeopardize this work
Which is there to serve spiritual goals.
Without the advice and help you give, I would be lamed.
Consider also what a deep and earnest sense of duty
Must arise when destiny gives such a clear sign,
As I have to recognize, in the gathering together of these people.

Manager

The more you go on like this,
The more you convince me that
You've fallen into error, and don't even know it.
You think you are serving humanity:
In fact you're only serving the little circle of people
Who, because of your support, will be able
To devote themselves for a little longer
To their spirit-dream.
This place will soon be bustling with activity,
Which these souls will no doubt see as 'spiritually ordained';
In fact it will be a phantom of hot air,
Which will eat up all the hard-earned fruits of our work.

Hilary   If you will not offer me your support,
             The future does indeed appear bleak.

                 Enter Strader

             Ah, dear Strader, I've been expecting you…
             What's just transpired makes it necessary
             For us to postpone our outing,
             And to discuss certain important matters instead.
             My old friend has just confided in me
             That he cannot go along with what we're planning.
             So let us now hear from the man
             Who has fully committed himself to our work.
             Much depends now on how people's souls
             May find one another; we confront each other
             Like different worlds, and yet we are asked
             To unite our strengths and thus create something
             Of great importance for the world.

Strader   So Hilary's entrusted colleague will not
             Support the hope-filled project, which
             Precisely your wisdom makes possible?
             But our plan will only then be able to succeed
             When well-tested practical experience
             Wisely joins with goals that serve the future.

Manager   I do not intend merely to withhold my support.
             I would also like to show to my good friend
             The complete pointlessness of what he's doing.

Strader   I'm not surprised that you should think
             That any plan that bears the name of 'Strader'
             Is doomed to failure.
             I've had to witness the collapse of an even greater project,
             Because the forces are still hidden in our time
             That have the power to make what's well-thought out
                 materially effective.

People know I have to thank spiritual illumination
For what did prove its validity, yet could not come to life.
This testifies for people against my powers of judgement
And at the same time kills their faith that the wellsprings
Of true creativity on earth are to be found in the spirit.

It will be hard, I know, for me to convince people
That through this experience I have gained the strength
To avoid making the same error twice.
I had to go wrong then, in order this time
To steer safely past truth's rocky cliffs.

Your doubts, though, are completely understandable.
Your kind of spirit, in particular, must find
Almost no value in the way we work.

But it is also said you wish to keep your working life
Strictly separate from a striving for the spirit,
Where we seek, through our own forces,
To work transformatively upon our souls,
You want to see that as a matter
Only for those times when we are not working.
To bring together, though, our inner, spiritual work
With the work we do in the physical world –
This is the goal of that spiritual stream
Which has clearly shown to me
The way life must develop.

Manager   For as long as we offer up what we attain in spirit
Only to the spirit,
Our souls are ennobled and our lives
Find their meaning.
But when spirit also wishes to experience existence
And even to master other realities than its own,
It approaches realms where

Truth is often threatened by illusion.
I've gained this insight through my own efforts in
    understanding spiritual matters.
And it is this that has formed my attitude today –
Not my natural inclinations, as you've wrongly assumed
From what others have said of me.

Strader   So then it is a *spiritual* error in you
Which makes you oppose my views with such hostility.
Our difficulties will therefore grow ever greater.
It's relatively easy for the spiritual researcher
To work in partnership with other human beings,
Who have let themselves be instructed
By nature and by life, about the meaning of existence.
But when thoughts, which claim to spring
From spiritual sources,
Come into conflict with others when they attempt to unite –
Then harmony can seldom be achieved.

============

(*After musing in silence:*)
Yet … whatever must happen, will happen.
Please – make a new examination of my plans.
Perhaps it will make you change
The opinion that you formed of them at first.

Curtain, while each remains fixed in thought.

Scene II

A mountain landscape. In the background, Hilary's house in the vicinity of the factory, though the factory is not visible. On the right – a waterfall. Johannes and, unknown to him, Capesius.

Johannes   Rock walls, rising steeply from the earth –
Towering up… their silent being
Fills all space, creating vast riddles.
It does not mortify the soul, in an agony of questioning,
That does not wish to understand the revelation of existence,
But only to gaze upon it
And drink in its living blessing.
Around these rocks ... the flickering play of light –
Their bare, flat surfaces ... their silent strength.
And here, the forest... green shades darkening into blue.
This is the world in which Johannes' soul
Weaving for itself images of the future,
Would happily linger.

          ============

Johannes' soul must feel within itself
The depths and widths of this majestic world.
Creative powers will then release in him
Capacities to reveal to human hearts
The magic of the world, transformed through art.

Johannes would be capable of none of this, though,
If not for Maria, whose tender warmth
Awoke, so lovingly, the forces of his soul.
I thank the wise guidance of destiny
For bringing me so near to her.
What a brief time since I've known her
Present at my side; what a deep union
Has been formed, in these few weeks,
Between my soul and hers.

Her spirit lives in me, even when she's far away;
When I call up before my soul the deepest strivings of my will,
It is she who thinks within my thinking.

Maria appears as a thought-form of Johannes.

Maria, here in front of me? But in what form?
She should never appear to me like this.
So spiritually stern – so 'worthy' –
Freezing all earthly feeling – no –
Johannes cannot – will not –
See Maria like this – It cannot be the same Maria
That wise powers of destiny
So gently led towards me.

Maria vanishes from Johannes's vision.

Where is the Maria who had such love for Johannes –
Before she had transformed his soul
And led it into frosty heights of spirit?

And also the Johannes – who loved Maria –
Where is he now? He was here a moment ago.
Blissfully restoring me to myself.
But he's vanished. The past
Cannot so cruelly wrench him from me.

Maria again becomes visible to Johannes.

Maria   Maria, as you wish to see her,
           Does not exist in worlds where truth prevails.
           The spirit of Johannes, waylaid by soul-delusions,
           Wanders into realms of untruth; free yourself
           From the power of your wishes, which tempt you.
           The raging storm of your soul I feel within me;
           It robs me of the peace I need.
           It is not Johannes who sends this storm into my soul;
           But a being he has long since overcome within himself.

It wanders now, in phantom-form, through widths of
   spirit-space.
Recognize it! And it will dissolve into nothingness.

Johannes   This is Maria – in truth.
She speaks about Johannes as at this time
He really does appear to himself.
Long ago he raised himself to a state of being
Quite different from what the fantastic play of dreams
Paints for me, as I have allowed my soul
To be lulled into a peaceful, drowsy twilight state.
But this dreamy state does not yet possess me.
I can still flee from it – and want to now.
It often draws me into its orbit – and then it seeks,
With all its strength, to wholly win me for itself – ;
But it drives me to free myself from it.
For years it has filled me, in the depths of my soul,
With spirit-substance –
And yet –
I do not wish to know it any more.

You alien being in Johannes' soul –
Leave me! Give me back to myself, as I once was –
Before you began to work within me.
I wish to see Johannes
Wholly freed from you. – –

Benedictus, also as a thought-form of Johannes, appears beside Maria.

Benedictus   Johannes, heed the voice of warning in your soul!
The One fills you spiritually, who has arisen
Now as the primary power of your being,
He must faithfully hold sway, at your side,
Demanding of you that, within your will,
You fashion into human form the forces of his being.
Hidden within you he must work

So that one day you may become
What you know already to be your far future goal.
Your personal struggles you must bear through life,
Shut tight within your soul. You yourself
You will only win, when you let yourself,
Courageously, be ever more fully possessed by him.

Maria (*seen as a thought of Johannes*)
My solemn holy vow rays out its strength,
Which shall preserve for you what you've achieved.
You find me in the frozen fields of ice,
Where spirits must themselves create the light
When darknesses may lame the powers of life. –
Seek for me in depths of worlds, where souls
Must battle to attain the feeling of the gods,
Through victories that win from nothingness new being.
But never seek me in the shadowy realm
Where tattered soul-remnants win, from delusory being,
A fleeting life – and where the spirit is wrapped
In a fantastic play of dreams,
Because it seeks oblivion in self-enjoyment
And *seriousness* seems too much trouble.

(*Benedictus and Maria disappear.*)

Johannes   She speaks of delusion ----
----- But how beautiful it is!
It is alive; Johannes feels himself within it.
Within it he also feels the nearness of Maria.
Johannes has no desire to know how the spirit
Solves riddles in dark depths of soul.
But he does want to create – and to work as an artist.
So, let there still stay hidden for him
That which, were it conscious,
Would *only* wish to gaze on higher worlds.

He sinks into further contemplation. Capesius gets up from his seat, shaking himself as if from profound contemplation.

Capesius   Have I not just clearly experienced, in my own soul,
            The images of longing created, almost
            In a dream, by Johannes?
            Thoughts flared up within me, that
            Did not come from me; --- which only he could have.
            The being of his soul lived in mine.
            I saw his younger self, as he deludedly
            Saw himself in spirit and frivolously
            Shunned the ripe fruits of his spirit. ---

            But how? Why am I experiencing this now?
            It is no ordinary happening for the spirit researcher
            To behold the soul of another within oneself!

            I've often heard from Benedictus
            That only they can do this – for a short time –
            Who have been singled out, by grace of destiny,
            In order to be raised up *one step higher*
            On their spiritual path. ----
            Can I think that this applies to me?
            Something that *may* only happen rarely,
            For it would be terrible if at any time
            The seer could eavesdrop on other people's souls!

            ============

            Did I see the truth? --- Or was it delusion
            That let me dream of another soul?
            I must find out from Johannes himself.

Capesius approaches Johannes who now becomes aware of him.

Johannes   Capesius – I thought that you were miles away.

Capesius   My soul felt very near to yours.

Johannes   Near to mine – in this moment – it can't have done!

Capesius   Why are you so shocked?

Johannes   No, no… I'm not shocked ---

Enter Maria

Johannes (*to himself*)
     --- His gaze … He really does see right through me.

Capesius (*to himself*)
     His shock shows me that I've seen the truth.

     (*He turns to Maria*)

     Maria, you've appeared at the right moment.
     Perhaps you can solve the heavy riddle weighing on me.

Maria   I didn't expect to find you here, but Johannes.
     Sensing that he was wrestling with some great riddle
     I came to look for him – you, though,
     I imagined at peace, contemplating
     The beautiful goals of the project
     That Hilary now makes possible.

Capesius   Beautiful goals? What are they to me?
     They're just a burden now.

Maria   A burden? But you were so happy
     That this was just what you were hoping for?

Capesius   What I have experienced in this hour of destiny
     Has wrought a complete change in me –
     Any kind of earthly activity would now damage
     The powers of seership that have awoken in me.

Maria   Whoever has been able to walk on paths of spirit
     Experiences many such destiny-laden signs. –
     He must follow them, in soul;
     But he cannot have interpreted them rightly
     If they turn his earthly duties into a burden.

Capesius sits and falls briefly into a state of contemplation.
Lucifer appears to Maria.

Lucifer   All your efforts are in vain.
                Within his heart, powers are at work
                Which allow me entrance to his soul.
                Maria – direct your seership
                Into his soul depths – you will see
                How with spirit-wings he lifts himself free
                From your work on earth, so filled with love and warmth.

Lucifer remains in the landscape. As Maria turns decisively to Capesius to
rouse him from his contemplation, he comes to himself of his own accord.

Maria   If Johannes, on his spirit-path,
                Was to feel burdened by his earthly duties,
                It wouldn't be justified – but it would be understandable:
                For his task is to create things, outwardly.
                But yours is to share spirit-knowledge with people,
                So you'll remain in the sphere of the soul.

Capesius   Spirit-power is lost far more in *words*
                Than in creating outer things.
                Words force us to use concepts for what we see;
                But concepts are enemies of seership.
                The spiritual experience I had
                Was only visible to my inner eye
                Because that soul that appeared to me,
                Though known to my earthly self,
                Has never been fully *grasped* by it. –
                If my experience proves true, then *nothing*
                Will hold me to this project.
                I will have to feel that lofty powers
                Point me now to other goals
                Than those Hilary has in mind.

Facing Johannes:

Johannes – speak plainly – just now,
When you were lost in contemplation,
Were you feeling long-past wishes of your soul
Arise again in you, like your present self?

Johannes   Is it possible then for my spirit's wild confusion
To reproduce itself and be the inner experience of someone else?
And does the seeing of it so strengthen the error
That it then becomes part of the wider world, outside us?

Johannes sinks again into contemplation. Maria turns her gaze to Lucifer and hears him speak.

Lucifer   I find the gates open to this soul as well!
I will use this situation well!
If this soul too is filled with spirit-wishes,
Then must the work of love,
Which through Hilary is now so dangerous for me,
Collapse and fail!
All Maria's power within Johannes I shall destroy.
Then everything she could achieve will fall to me!

Exit Lucifer. Capesius consciously straightens himself up and speaks with ever-greater confidence.

Capesius   There can be no doubt. I did see truly.
I was able to see what Johannes was living through.
It is also quite clear, that his world
Could only reveal itself to me, because mine
Has never sought to grasp his conceptually.
The spirit-path demands complete solitude.
Only those who encounter each other conceptually
Can work together. The soul can only reach
The wide spheres of the worlds of light
If it keeps itself far away from human life.

I find in Father Felix my example.
In proud solitude he seeks the spirit-light,
On pathways strange to other people.
And his search has been successful – because
He has always kept himself far away from conceptual life.
I shall continue to follow his path: and your work,
Where spirit-sight is burdened by earthly reality,
Will no longer tempt Capesius.

He leaves.

Maria   This is how it is with human beings
When their better self sinks into spirit-sleep,
And powers of wishes nourish them,
Until they are once more able to awaken,
Filling with light their true spirit-nature.
This is the sleep that all people sleep
Before they are awakened by spirit-sight.
They know nothing of this waking-sleeping,
They seem awake – because they always sleep.
Whenever the seer moves from his true state of being
To such a kind of waking, he falls asleep.
Capesius will now leave us.
It's no passing whim, but his whole condition,
Which drives him away from our goals.
That he turns away from us, is not his doing.
One sees in it powerful signs of destiny.
The rest of us must therefore devote ourselves
To the work even more strongly.

Johannes   Maria, don't demand of Johannes, right now,
That he steel himself for new goals.
Like Capesius, his soul needs spirit-sleep,
So it may ripen its quietly germinating forces.
One day, I know, I will make myself strong enough
To work for spirit-worlds, – but don't ask now

That I become active – not now!
It was me, remember, who drove Capesius away.
If I had been ready for this work, he would be as well.

Maria   You drove Capesius away? You must be dreaming!

Johannes I dreamed quite knowingly –
Yes, I dreamed while wide awake.
What to cosmic powers is but semblance
Showed itself to me as a completely clear image
Of where I am in my development.
I know for sure: my wishing, my desiring, was my very self.
And so Johannes was present in my soul
As he used to be, before his spirit seized hold of him
And filled him with that second self.
He is not dead; Johannes' life of wishing and desiring
Renders him the companion of my soul.
Though I have dazed him, I have not conquered him.
He demands the right to his own existence
Every time that second self….. must fall asleep.
And always to stay awake – is too much for it.
And so it was sleeping in that moment
When Capesius experienced within himself
How that other being tore me from myself.
And so the power that drove him away
Is at work in me and not in him – the power
That will not allow us
To turn our spirits to this earthly work.

Maria   The spirit-powers draw near – call on them!
Turn your gaze to depths of spirit-worlds.
And wait, until the powers at work there
Feel what it is, in your own true being,
That moves in affinity with theirs.
They will conjure you up, before your spirit-eye,
Enabling you and them to become one.

And the spirit in you will speak with spirit-beings;
Listen closely to this spirit-conversation.
It will bear you into spheres of light
And bind you, in your essence, to the spirit.
What is dimly glimmering to you now, from far distant times,
You will see quite clearly, in the light of the world.
It will exert no power over you,
For you will freely direct it.
Compare it with the elemental beings,
With different kinds of shadows and spectres.
Place it next to every kind of demon
And you'll experience what it really is.
But come to know yourself in realms of spirits
Who join together Primal world-beginnings;
Who know their nearness to the fountain-springs of life;
And give direction to the spheres' wise aims.
Such cosmic vision will so strengthen you
That, amidst the surging waves of spirit,
You will be able to unite that which lives
In the very core of your soul, with yourself.

============

It is the spirit's will I tell you this.
Just listen then to what you have been conscious of
And yet, till now, have not been wholly wedded to,
In depths of soul.

Johannes (*clearly showing that he has roused himself to a strong decision.*)
     I will hear it – in spite of myself – I will!

From both sides of the stage enter elemental beings.
From stage-right – small, steel-grey, gnome-like beings. They are nearly all head,
which droops forward, and they have long, mobile limbs, well adapted for
gesturing but clumsy for walking.
From stage-left – slim, nearly headless, sylph-like forms, their feet and hands
something between fins and wings. Some of them are yellow-red with sharply-

outlined figures; the others are blue-green and less defined.
The words spoken by all these beings are accompanied by expressive gestures,
which develop into dance.

Chorus of Gnomes

> We harden, we strengthen
> The glittering, dusty matter.
> We loosen, we crumble
> The stiff and crusty strata.
> We nimbly crush the hard-stuff,
> And slowly fasten loose-stuff,
> With bodies made of spirit
> And woven out of thinking-matter –
> Already quick and clever,
> When sleepy human beings
> At earth's beginning still were dreaming.

Chorus of Sylphs

> We weave, we unravel
> The airy water-surges.
> We sunder, we scatter
> The living sun-force in the seed.
> With care we thicken powers of light,
> And lessen wisely force of fruiting,
> With bodies, soul-enwoven
> And flowing out from radiant feeling,
> Which ever-living glimmers,
> That human beings living
> Find joy in earth-becoming's meaning.

Chorus of Gnomes

> We laugh and we chuckle,
> We mock and we snigger,
> When human beings stumbling,
> With human senses fumbling,
> Perceive what we've created

And think their brains can comprehend it.
When really spirits working
Have conjured it before their stupid staring.

Chorus of Sylphs

We nurture, we cherish,
We ripen, we quicken,
When children into life first entering,
When aged ones in error weaving,
Are nourished by our workings;
And children and the aged ones
All dim enjoy within time's streaming
What we eternally are pondering.

*These elemental beings form two clusters and remain visible in the background.
From stage-right the three soul-forces appear – Philia, Astrid and Luna – with
the 'Other Philia'.*

Philia

They ray forth their brightness
As lights filled with loving
That blessedly ripen;
They warm with their mildness
They heat with great power,
As the world of becoming
Seeks effectual being;
That effectual being
Brings souls joy and delight
Who with love do surrender
To the radiant light.

Astrid

They weave what is living
As fashioning helpers
In arising of being.
The earths they burst open
The airs they fast thicken,
That there be transformation
In creation's great striving.

That creation's great striving
Makes happy the spirits
Who feel themselves weaving
In the life of creation.

Luna   They're carefully moulding
As active creators,
The malleable matter;
The edges they sharpen
The surfaces smoothen,
That rightly be builded
The forms as they stand there;
That forms as they stand there
Enthuse people's wills
For right ways to build
As active creators.

The Other Philia
They pluck all the blossoms
As wild carefree users
And work like enchanters;
They dream all that's truthful
Uphold all delusion;
That the seed which is sleeping
Be awakened to life;
For now waking dreaming
To souls is revealing
Enchantment that's weaving
Throughout their own being.

The four soul-forces leave stage-left, together with the elemental beings. Johannes, who during the previous events, was sunk in deep contemplation, arouses himself from it.

Johannes   "For now waking dreaming
To souls is revealing
Enchantment that's weaving

Throughout their own being."
These words still clearly sound within me –
All that I was seeing, though,
Has fled from my soul in chaos. ----

But what power is it that stirs in me when I ponder:
Enchantment that's weaving
Throughout their own being. –

He falls again into meditation. Before him, as his own thought-form, there appears the Spirit of Johannes's Youth, with Lucifer at its left side, and the soul of Theodora at its right side.

Spirit of Johannes's Youth

    Your wishes and desires, they feed my life,
    My breath drinks deep the dreaming of your youth;
    When you make no attempt to enter worlds
    Where I can't follow – then I exist.
    But when you lose me in yourself
    Then I in pain must serve cruel shades
    And do their dreadful work.
    Sustainer of my life – do not abandon me!

Lucifer

    He will not abandon you – I see desires
    For light within his being's depths
    Which cannot follow in Maria's footsteps. –
    When these desires, with all the glory they give rise to,
    Fully illumine Johannes's creative soul:
    He will not wish to see their precious fruits
    Be squandered in that realm
    Where Love alone holds sway, without Beauty.
    Then he'll no longer prize that self so highly
    That, by over-estimating knowledge,
    Seeks to throw away its best forces to the shades.
    When wisdom's light starts shining in his wishes
    Their worth for him will fully be revealed;

They'll have but little value for him
While they remain submerged in darkness.
Until his wishes reach the light of wisdom,
It will be me who will sustain you – loyally –
With that light found deep in human souls.

Johannes still lacks pity for your sufferings,
Each time he strives to gain his light-filled heights
He always lets you sink among the shades.
And then he can forget that you, his child,
Must undergo your spell-bound life, of pain.
But from now on, I'll be there at your side
When you, a shadow, shiver through his guilt.
And I, Lucifer, by ancient right
(*The Spirit of Johannes's Youth winces at the word 'Lucifer'*)
Will seize for myself, in the depths of his soul,
What he leaves unguarded
In his flight to the spirit.
This treasure I'll then bring to you
To make lighter your dark solitude
In the world of shadows.
But you will only be fully freed from enchantment
When he can once again unite with you.
He can put this off – but not prevent it.
For Lucifer will have his ancient rights.

Theodora   You spirit-child – in the dark realm of the shades
You live out Johannes's youth. From realms, though,
Warmed through by love and filled with light,
The soul who protects Johannes lovingly leans
Towards you. She wishes to redeem you from enchantment –
If you are willing to receive from her feeling
That which will give you a life in blessedness.
I would join you with the beings of the elements,
Who work unconsciously in the surrounding world,

And always keep away from wakefulness of soul.
You can fashion forms with spirits of the earth
And shine out forces with the souls of fire,
If you'll offer up your knowing life unto that Will
Whose light, which has no human wisdom,
Shines with ever greater strength.
You'll keep your knowing, which is but half your own,
Safe from Lucifer, and be of most valuable
Service to Johannes. From the being of his soul
I will bring you what makes him thirst for your existence,
And reaches out to him refreshingly
The gift of spirit-sleep.

Lucifer   But *beauty* she can never give you –
             Which I will dare to snatch from her.

Theodora   I will let beauty spring from noble feeling –
             And ripen in the work of sacrifice.

Lucifer   She'll tear away from you your free will
             And give it to the spirits who rule in darkness.

Theodora   I will awaken that spirit-filled vision
             That knows it is even free from Lucifer.

*Lucifer, Theodora and the Spirit of Johannes's Youth disappear. Johannes,
awakening from meditation, sees the 'Other Philia' approaching him.*

The Other Philia
             For now waking dreaming
             To souls is revealing
             Enchantment that's weaving
             Throughout their own being.

Johannes   O mysterious spirit – it was your words
             That opened this world to me! –
             Yet only one of all its wonders seems important to me now.

That shadow that showed itself to me with Lucifer
    and Theodora –
Is it to be found – in realms of spirit –
As a *living being*?

The Other Philia

It is *living* – yes – and is, through you, awakened to existence.
Just as everything shows itself in image-form
Within a mirror, when its surface is lit,
So must everything you see in spirit –
Before full maturity grants you the right to such vision –
Be mirrored livingly within the realm
Of half-waking spirit shadows.

Johannes   So it is only an *image* – thus mirrored through me?

The Other Philia

But an image that *lives* and will stay alive
As long as you hold fast
To a life once lived, within you –
That you may daze
But cannot yet, for sure, completely conquer.
Your awakening, Johannes, will be nothing but illusion,
Till you yourself redeem that shade
Given by your *guilt*, a trapped, enchanted life.

Johannes   How grateful I am to this spirit.
It brings me true advice ----
Which I *must follow*.

Slow curtain, while the 'Other Philia' and Johannes remain motionless.

Scene III

The same landscape as in the preceding scene. Magnus Bellicosus, Romanus,
Torquatus and Hilary enter from stage-left, deep in conversation.

Bellicosus   But if the Manager, in his stubbornness, will not bend,
             How can the work succeed
             That Hilary wishes to place
             In such loving service to the world?

Romanus   The objections raised by the Manager –
                   our friend's loyal colleague –
             Do not only carry weight with those who arrive at their opinions
             After considering the *outer* demands of life –
             Are they not also in tune with the Mystic's true opinion?

Bellicosus   But they have no place at all among those
             Who spiritually surround and support our goals.
             The pupils of Benedictus took over from us,
             In our Mystic work; – Hilary is now wishing
             To create for them a setting for their work,
             So that their spirit-fruits may come to maturity.
             Wise powers of destiny brought them together with us
             Within the Temple; our friend [Hilary]
             Is merely answering the call of spirit-duty
             That was made known to us within the Temple.

Romanus   But are you sure you understand correctly
             What the spirit commanded? Doesn't it make much more sense
             That Benedictus and his pupils
             Should keep themselves within the inner Temple
             And not yet tread the rough path
             That Hilary wants to lead them on?
             For even with him, spirit-vision can change all too easily
             To a sleep, where the soul but dreams.

Bellicosus	I'd have hoped never to hear you say such things!
	They might be said by Hilary's Manager
	Who only gains from books, the knowledge he has.
	But you are called upon to recognize the signs
	That show themselves upon the Mystic path.
	The manner in which Benedictus's pupils were led to us
	Speaks a clear language. They have been
	Brought together with us, so we may follow
	What is shown to their clairvoyance.
Torquatus	Another sign, though, shows
	That the full blessings of the Spirit-Powers
	Have not streamed down upon the work
	Placed before our souls within the Temple.
	Capesius has separated from Benedictus
	And his circle of pupils.
	The fact that he has not yet experienced
	Within himself the wakefulness of soul
	That Benedictus by now was hoping to find in him
	Casts serious doubts upon the teacher's reliability as well.
Bellicosus	Though I'm still far from the gifts of real seership,
	I will often feel how a certain event
	Unlocks an intuitive foreboding in me.
	The first time I saw Capesius, at his place in the Temple,
	The thought oppressed me that destiny had brought him
	Both near to us and far from us at the same time.
Romanus	I well understand this foreboding of yours.
	But the intuitive sense that I had at that moment
	Was that none of these new occult friends of ours
	Was so closely bound to me, by destiny, as Strader.
	For me such intuitive feeling is just a sign
	Pointing out to me the direction
	Where my thinking should set to work.
	But when it's time to turn to action

I must then eradicate this intuitive feeling
Empowering my thought.
The strict rules of occultism teach me this.
I do indeed feel closely connected to Benedictus's pupils
In the sphere of the spirit,
But if I am to find the way back
From this inner circle
To everyday life on earth,
Then only with *Strader*
Would I dare to do this.

Ahriman appears in the background and passes from stage-left to stage-right without being seen.

Torquatus   Hilary's Manager doesn't see Strader at all
As the sure spirit
Able to be effective in outer life.
And my own inner voice, if I listen to it,
Reveals that Strader completely lacks
The proper soul mood for mysticism.
What outer signs can convince him of,
What his own reasoning can grasp of life in the spirit,
Stir in him the powerful drive to do research.
But he's still a long way from direct spiritual experience.
How could such a person's spiritual creativity
Be anything else
Than a dark, mystical web of dreams?

Romanus   Up until now he has not gone far enough
Down the spirit-path of his friends
To have become linked to those opponents of the soul,
Which are of great danger to many a Mystic,
If they pursue him into sense-existence.

Bellicosus   If you believe him free of such opponents
Then nothing stands in the way of your helping him –
So that the great work Hilary

Wants to carry out through him
Can be achieved.
When the Manager hears how highly you revere Strader,
While he holds him in such low regard,
It will be sure to shake his confidence in his own judgement.
You alone are capable of winning him over.
He's well aware that
Owing to the way you cleverly will think things through
    beforehand,
Everything you've done in outer life
Has always been successful.

Romanus   My dear Hilary, if you place Strader at your side,
And, free of illusion, will keep the rest of Benedictus's pupils
Far away from your work,
You will no longer be on your own;
For I would then not only give you the help
That Bellicosus asks of me,
I would furthermore place everything I own at your disposal,
In order to serve, as effectively as I can,
Strader's beautiful plans.

Hilary   How can you possibly think that Strader would part now
From Benedictus's other pupils –
And without them simply seek his own spirit-goals?
The others are as *near* to him as his own self.

Romanus   They may, of course, be near to him, as people.
Only *that* part of his soul, though,
Which is still in deep spirit-sleep,
Could imagine that he is *spiritually* united to them as well.
Very soon, though, I think we'll see
How that sleeping part as well can *waken* into life.

*They exit stage-right. From the other side enter Capesius, Strader, Felix and
Felicia.*

Capesius   All I can do at present
              Is to follow the spirit inwardly, within my soul.
              Were I to take on the burden of outer work,
              Attempting to make the spirit manifest in the world of sense, –
              I'd have to pretend to grasp the ground of existence
              In worlds whose being
              Has not gained full reality as yet
              Within me.
              I can only behold as much of cosmic existence
              As takes on form *in me.*
              How can what I create help other people,
              If when I create it
              I am just indulging in myself.

Strader   What you are saying, if I understand you,
              Is that all that you would create
              Would bear the stamp of your own being;
              And that you'd therefore only be giving the world
              Your own self?

Capesius   Until my own inner world
              Bumps up against some other being,
              That's how it is.
              Just how little I'm yet able to enter the world of another,
              I had painfully to admit to myself,
              When recently I awoke for a brief moment to full clarity.

Felix Balde   I have never heard you say these things. –
              But – – I have never understood you as well
              As now, when nothing but your own self is speaking.
              There resounds through your words the true mood of mysticism,
              Which has been my discipline for many years.
              Only this can perceive the light
              In which, through clear vision,
              The human spirit can knowingly experience itself
              Within the cosmic spirit.

Capesius   Feeling how near I've come to you,
            I fled here to you from a commotion
            That would have killed my inner world.

Strader   In the past I often understood the things you're now saying – ;
            I saw them as wisdom, – – but *right now*
            Not a single word of it makes sense to me.
            Capesius and Father Felix – *they both*…
            Conceal dark meanings in clear words…

            I seem to be experiencing your words as just
            The outer clothing of certain soul-powers,
            Which drive me far away from you into worlds
            Quite distant from your kind of spirit.
            Worlds I don't wish for – because it is *your* worlds I have to love
            With my inmost soul.
            It's easy to bear the opposition
            Now threatening my work from outside.
            Yes – even if my whole will should be shattered
            In the face of it – I could endure.
            But to do without your worlds – this is impossible for me.

Felix Balde Human beings cannot find the spirit world
            If they attempt to enter it by *seeking*.
            It gave me great joy once, hearing you speak
            About your invention; –
            How what you did not want to achieve
            By seeking with your intellect
            You received as illumination.
            Then you were near mysticism's true mood.

            To strive for *nothing* – – only to be still and at peace,
            The inner being of the soul wide open – – ;
            That is the mystic mood. – Whoever can *awaken* it,
            Leads their inmost soul to the realm of Light.
            Outer work makes such a mood impossible.

             If through mysticism you try and accomplish outer work,
             With mystic delusions you'll destroy your life.

Strader   I need you both – but I cannot find you –.
             That which unites us – you see no value in.
             How can people ever find each other, to work for the world,
             If mystics refuse to step beyond their own beings.

Felix Balde   The realities of vision are fragile and tender.
             Were you to carry them
             Into the world of your activity and work,
             They would dissolve into nothing
             As you passed across.
             In devout reverence for the spirit-powers that hold sway,
             Allowing spirit-vision to be at peace within the heart –
             Only thus do mystics near the world of *action*.

Capesius   And should they attempt to enter it some other way,
             It will show them very well how error works within it,
             But not the glorious, light-filled being of wisdom.
             I was able to see into someone else's soul –
             I know my inner sight did not deceive me.
             But I only saw the error of that soul.
             This was all I could see, as by wishing for outer deeds
             I had spoiled my spirit-sight.

Strader   Thus speaks Capesius, who treads the path
             Far in advance of me.
             And yet, for *me*, spiritual vision only arises
             When I devote myself to thoughts
             Of what can be achieved through deeds.
             And then I find myself alive with hope
             That I may build up places
             Where the spirit can enkindle light –
             Light which warmly streams through worlds of spirit
             And seeks through human activity in the senses' world
             A new home on the earth.

Am I a child of error, then – not your child –
You wisdom-filled worlds of the spirit – – !

Strader turns away just for a moment from the others. He has the following spirit-vision – Benedictus, Ahriman and Maria appear as Strader's thought-forms – but he is nonetheless in genuine spiritual communication with them. (At first Benedictus with Ahriman, then Maria.)

Benedictus   In wisdom-filled worlds of the spirit
You seek relief from the pain your question brings.
A pain that makes the deepest riddle of your inner life
Weigh heavily on your earthly thinking.
You shall hear the answer – from the depths of your soul,
As the wide worlds of the spirit wish to reveal through my voice.
But learn to grasp what you believe that you know,
What you very often have the courage to speak out,
But which you do but dream,
Within your own soul.
Give to your dream the *life* I am called on

     Ahriman appears.

To reach out to you from the spirit.
What your thinking, though,
Can draw out from the realm of the senses,
This must be transformed into dream-existence.
Capesius and Father Felix
Are banishing you from the spirit-light that they behold.
They open up an abyss between themselves and you.
Do not regret that they have done this –
But gaze into your own abyss.

Ahriman   Just do it!
You will behold what of the human spirit
You find valuable in the world's wide course.
It would be better if other spirits showed this to you

While you were in a dull soul-sleep.
But Benedictus shows it to you while you're awake,
So you'll kill the answer you receive, by seeing it.
Yes. Just do it!

Strader   I will do it. But how?
Confused forms... Shifting and changing...
Tearing... Tearing at one another... A war!
Spectres hurling themselves on one another...
Destruction reigns... generating darkness all around;
From the darkness other shadows.
Around them an etheric radiance... reddish... weaving;
One of the forms – quite clearly – frees itself;
Approaches me – sent to me by the abyss.

Maria appears out of the abyss.

Maria   You are seeing demons;
Take hold of your strength – and they will change.
They appear to you as they are not.
If you can hold them fast,
Until their spectral beings shine before your soul,
You'll see the value they can have within the world's evolving.
Your vision fades away, though,
Before they find the strength to shine.
Illumine them with your own light.
Where is your light?
You radiate darkness.
Recognize your own darkness around you –
You're creating wild confusing darkness in the light.
You experience it, as it arises,
But never experience yourself creating it.
You want to forget your craving to create.
But it rules, unconsciously, within your being,
Because you are too cowardly to radiate your light.
You want to enjoy this light of yours.

You want to enjoy *yourself alone* within it.
You are seeking for yourself – and are seeking through forgetting.
You are letting yourself sink, dreaming, into yourself.

Ahriman Yes, hear her – she can solve your riddles.
But *her* solution will be no solution for *you*!
She gives you wisdom –
So you can make your way with it to folly!
It could be good for you – in future –
In the bright light of spirit-day;
But when Maria speaks to you like this within your dreams,
She kills the solution, even as she gives it.
Hear her!

Strader What do these words want, Maria?
Have they been born from the light?
From *my* light? Or do they sound out
From my darkness? Benedictus, speak:
Who was it who rose up out of the abyss
To give me counsel?

Benedictus She came to find you at your own abyss.
Thus do spirits seek out human beings, to protect them
From beings who fashion spectres before their souls.
These spread such confusing darkness
Over the ruling of the World Spirit
That human beings only have knowledge of themselves
Within the web of their own being.
Gaze deeper into your own abyss!

Strader What is it I see living now, in the depths of the abyss?

Benedictus Behold the shadow-beings:
To the right, the bluish-red ones, tempting Felix.
And the others, to the left – red, gently brightening into yellow –
Pressing in upon Capesius.
They both feel the power of these shadows – – ;

And in their loneliness, each creates for himself
The light that lames the shadows of deceit.

Ahriman

He would do better if he showed you
Your shadows.
But he's not capable of it.
It's not that he's lacking in good will.
He just doesn't notice where to look for them.
They're standing right behind you, perilously near.
But you yourself are hiding them from him!

Strader

So here at the abyss I hear the same words
I found so foolish
When Hilary's Manager spoke them.

Maria

Father Felix tempers the weapons he needs
To ward off his dangers.
But other weapons are needed
By one who has to walk your soul-paths.
And the sword Capesius is forging for himself –
To bravely fight against his soul's opponents –
For you would become a shadow-sword,
If you would use it in that spiritual battle
Souls cannot avoid
Who have to powerfully transform their spirit-being
To make them ripe for earthly deeds.
Their weapons are of no use to you.
But you must know them,
In order to forge, in the right way,
From soul-substance, your own.

The forms of Benedictus, Ahriman and Maria disappear. Outwardly speaking, in other words, Strader returns from his spiritual vision; he looks around for Capesius, Felix and Felicia; they come over to him again; he has meanwhile sat down on a rock.

Felix Balde   My dear Strader. Weren't you transported
                Far away from us just now in spirit...
                That's how it seemed.

He pauses. When Strader does not reply, he continues.

                I had no wish to heartlessly
                Drive you away from us
                Onto other paths of life.
                But only to prevent you yielding even more
                To the power of delusion muddling you.
                What is perceived in the spirit should only spiritually
                Be experienced and received.
                Think of the beings of Felicia's fairy-tales.
                They are living in her soul
                And only in people's *souls* do they wish to be experienced.
                How foolish it would be if she wanted to
                Le them dance about on puppet-stages!
                All their magic would be gone.

Felicia Balde I really have been silent long enough!
                But I must speak, when you even want to make my fairy-folk
                Happy – with your 'mystic mood'.
                How thankful they would be,
                When after sucking from them all their power
                You then with mysticism puff them back to life.
                All respect to mysticism, of course; but please –
                Keep it far away from my fairy-tale realms!

Capesius   Felicia, was it not your fairy-tales
                That first set me on the spirit-path?
                The air and water spirits
                You so often summoned up before my thirsting soul –
                Were the first messengers to me from that world
                Which now, upon the mystic path, I seek to enter.

Felicia Balde But since you've been coming to our house

With your new 'mystic ways' –
You ask but little
Of what my beautiful magic beings want.
The ones with a solemn and worthy look
You'll still let pass
But those who, full of joy, love dancing wildly,
Appear to disturb your mystic feelings.

Capesius No doubt, Felicia, the deeper meaning of those wonderful beings,
Who display their earnestness in such playful masks
Will also one day be revealed to me.
For now, though, it is beyond my strength.

Felix Balde Felicia, you know how I love them,
Your fairy-folk, that appear to you;
But to imagine them mechanically embodied
As puppets – I find repulsive.

Felicia Balde I haven't presented them yet to you in this way.
I know that you are above such things!
But I was happy when I heard of what Strader is planning
And learned that Johannes, too,
Was striving to clothe the spirit in sense-perceptible form.
I could see in the spirit my fairy-tale princes – my fire-souls too –
Joyfully dancing, with such beauty in their art,
In thousands of plays for puppets.
So I've already let them –
With delight at the thought of it –
Seek out the playrooms
Of many, many children.

Curtain.

Scene IV

The same landscape as in the two preceding scenes. The Manager and Romanus are speaking with one another during a walk.

(Later: Johannes, Johannes's Double, the Spirit of Johannes's Youth; the Guardian of the Threshold, Ahriman; Benedictus, Maria; Strader, the soul of Theodora.)

Manager   You are someone who knows well Hilary's mystic friends
And I see in you an intelligent man –
Who always keeps watch over his power of judgement,
Both with regard to working life and to concerns of the spirit.
I therefore value your opinion.
But how am I to understand what you've just said?
It seems right to you that Strader's friends
Should keep themselves within the realm of the spirit,
And not yet use their powers of seership
To work in practical life.
But isn't this just as dangerous for Strader?
His whole spiritual approach seems to me to prove
That nature-demons constantly delude him,
When he acts upon his strong desire
To work, through deeds, in outer life.
The wise pupil of the spirit knows
That he must first strengthen himself inwardly
Before he can resist such demons.
But Strader, on his spirit-path, seems completely unaware
Of such opponents.

Romanus   But those good spirit-beings, who guide people
Still outside the spirit, have not yet left his side.
These good spirits turn away from Mystics, though,
When they link themselves to beings that serve
Their special Mystic Mood.
In Strader's bearing, I can quite clearly feel
How nature-demons are still blessing him
With the fruits of their *good* forces.

Manager So nothing except your own *feelings* convince you
         Of the good spirits in Strader!
         You offer so little – and demand so much!
         I suppose I too should consult these spirits
         If I'm to continue working here! –
         Where for so long I've been allowed
         To serve the work and its *true spirit*,
         Which was so dear to Hilary's father.
         It still speaks to me from the old man's grave,
         Even if his son no longer cares to listen to it.
         What would the spirit of that virtuous man say
         If he could see the muddle-headed minds
         His son is trying to bring into the firm?
         I know this spirit, that for ninety years
         Maintained itself within his body.
         It taught me the true mysteries of work,
         In the days when it was still actively involved within the business,
         While the son would creep away to the Mystics' Temple.

Romanus My friend, surely you must know
         How highly I esteem that spirit.
         That old man, who you have rightly made your example,
         So clearly served it.
         And from my childhood to the present
         I too have striven to serve it.
         Yet, I also crept off to the Mystics' Temple.
         I faithfully planted into the depths of my soul
         All that they wished to bestow on me.
         But my reasoning mind, when it then stepped back into life,
         Left the mood of the Temple behind.
         I knew that this was the best way
         To let the power of this mood work into earthly life.
         For you see, I *did* bring my *soul*
         Out of the Temple into my work.
         And the soul is best left
         Undisturbed by earthly reason.

Manager	And do you think that Strader's way of working

Manager   And do you think that Strader's way of working
Is even remotely similar to yours?
With you, I always know myself completely free
Of the spirit-beings Strader brings with him.
When he speaks – even when he's in error,
I feel how elemental spirits, burgeoning with life,
Pour themselves through his words and his whole being,
Revealing things inaccessible to our senses.
And it's precisely *this* I feel so repelled by.

Romanus   What you are saying strikes a deep chord in me.
Since I've drawn nearer to Strader,
I've had to feel how the thoughts I receive from him
Are endowed with quite extraordinary power.
They take living hold of me as if they were my own.
Then one day I had to ask myself:
What if you owe to *him* – and not *yourself* –
The force that has made you who you are?
This feeling was soon followed by another:
Do I owe everything that makes me useful in working life
And in the service of humanity
To a former life on earth?

Manager   He makes me feel exactly the same way.
As one draws nearer to him,
The spirit working through him
Powerfully draws in one's soul.
If a soul as strong as yours could succumb to him,
How should I protect my own
If I unite with him in work?

Romanus   It will depend entirely on you, whether you can find
The right way to relate to him.
For myself, I believe that Strader's power
Is not able to harm me,
Since I have formed thoughts
About how he may have attained that power.

Manager	Attained power – *him* – over you! The dreamer – over *you*, the master of the arts of life!
Romanus	One might, perhaps, dare to imagine That in Strader a spirit is living Who in an earlier life on earth Could raise himself to extraordinary heights of soul;-- Who knew much that other people Could as yet have no inkling of. Were this the case, it would then be quite possible That thoughts, that originated in his spirit, Then found their way Into the general life of mankind, Enabling people like myself To acquire their capacities in life. The thoughts I seized on in my youth In my environment, and made my own, Might well have sprung from this same spirit.
Manager	Does it really seem justified to you To attribute thoughts – of such tremendous value in life – Quite specifically to Strader?
Romanus	You know I am not a dreamer. I am not blindly spinning Some web of dreams About what influences our lives. Nor has it ever been my way To sleepily follow obscure thoughts. I look at Strader quite objectively; How he bears himself as an individual – With all his qualities – and how he acts; Even at what doesn't bear fruit in him. And it's quite clear to me That I had to form Exactly that judgement

Of his extraordinary gifts
That I have just described to you.
I feel him standing before me now in the spirit,
Just as if he'd already stood like this before me,
Many centuries ago.
In saying this – I know with certainty that I'm awake.
I will remain by Hilary's side.
What must happen, *will* happen.
Please think over his plans more deeply.

Manager   It's more important for me now
To think over what you've just confided in me.

Manager and Romanus walk on further into the landscape – they exit.
Johannes enters from another direction, deep in thought, and sits on a rock.

Johannes   I was astonished when Capesius disclosed
How my inner life of soul revealed itself to his spirit-sight.
What had been shown to me many years ago in a clear light
Had therefore become dark in me:
That all that lives in human souls
Continues working in the outer realms of the spirit –
I have known this for years already ... and yet I could *forget* it.
When Benedictus opened the path for me
To my first powers of spirit-sight,
I beheld in clear spirit-images
Capesius and Strader at other ages of their lives.
I saw how the strong forms created by their thinking
Caused rippling waves that spread through world-existence.
I know this very well – but didn't know it
When shown me by Capesius.
The 'knowing' part of me was fast asleep.
I've even known for years
How closely bound up I was
With Capesius in a long-past life on earth.
But in that moment I had no knowledge of this.
How can I guard within me what I know?

A Voice from the Distance – that of Johannes' Double
            Enchantment that's weaving
            Throughout their own being.

Johannes   For now waking dreaming
                  To souls is revealing
                  Enchantment that's weaving
                  Throughout their own being.

While Johannes is speaking, his double approaches him. Johannes does not recognize him, believing him to be the 'Other Philia'.

Johannes   You're there again – mysterious spirit.
                  You – who brought me true advice.

Double   Your awakening, Johannes, will be nothing but illusion,
                  Till you yourself redeem that shade
                  Given, by your *guilt*, a trapped, enchanted life.

Johannes   For the second time you speak these words
                  Which I will follow. Show me how to do so.

Double   Johannes, what is lost now within yourself –
                  Let it live – in the realm of the shades.
                  But so that it must not suffer pain –
                  Give it light from your own spirit-light.

Johannes   I may have dazed this shadow-being
                  But have not conquered him. Among the shades
                  He therefore must remain a trapped, enchanted being,
                  Until I re-unite myself with him.

Double   Then give to *me* all that you owe this being:
                  The power of love that draws your soul towards him,
                  The hope that he engendered in your heart,
                  The fresh new springs of life concealed within him,
                  The ripened fruits of long-past lives on earth
                  Which have been lost to you – by losing him –
                  O give them all to *me* – and I'll be sure – to bring them all to *him*.

Johannes	You know the way to him? Then show it to me!
Double	I once could reach him in the realm of shades.
	Each time you raised yourself to spirit-spheres;
	But since you have been lured – by powers that work in wishes –
	My strength fails, whenever I try to reach him.
	But if you now will follow my advice
	This strength may grow and recreate itself.
Johannes	I've given you my oath – that I would follow you.
	I give it once again, you riddling spirit –
	With the whole force of my soul.
	But if indeed you *can* find the way to him,
	Then *show* it to me too – in this fateful hour.
Double	I find it in this moment, but cannot guide you.
	All I can do is bring before your eyes of soul
	The being that your longing seeks.

The Spirit of Johannes's Youth appears.

Spirit of Johannes's Youth

> I will be always bounden to that spirit
> Who could open your eyes of soul,
> So that when, in future, I show myself to you, by spirit-law,
> Your vision may find me.
> But you must know who this spirit truly is
> By whose side you now do see me.

The Spirit of Johannes's Youth disappears. Only now does the Double become recognizable to Johannes.

Johannes	Not that mysterious spirit? ... My other self!
Double	Follow me... follow... as you gave me your oath;
	I now must lead you to my sovereign Lord.

The Guardian of the Threshold appears and stands beside the Double.

Guardian	Johannes, if you would free this spirit-shadow

From worlds of soul where it's enchanted,
Then kill the wishes leading you astray.
The trail that you are following disappears
As long as you keep searching with wishes and desire.
The trail, it leads you by my threshold,
But here, as is decreed by higher beings,
I must confuse the eyes of soul,
When wishes mingle with the spirit-glances,
Which only when they have met me
Can reach the pure light of Truth.

     Ahriman enters.

I'll find you out yourself, within your glance
And hold you fast
If you approach with wishes and desire.
The image you have of me as well
Can only be delusion
While the deluding power of wishes
Informs your gaze
And before spirit-peacefulness, like a soul-body,
Has won mastery of your whole being.
Make strong the words of power that you know
So that their spirit-force
Can conquer your delusion.
Recognize me then – *free of your own wishes;*
And you will see the true form of my being.
No longer will I need to check your vision
Which you may then turn freely to the spirit-realms.

Johannes   Even *you* then, I'm only seeing as an illusory image?
Even you – who I must see truly
Before I can see other beings within the spirit-world.
How can I hope to know the Truth
If with each further step, I only ever find One Truth:
That the web of delusion I spin grows ever thicker.

Ahriman   Then do not let him utterly confuse you!
He guards his threshold faithfully enough,
Even if he wears the clothes
That you yourself patched together in your mind
From bits and pieces of old melodramas.
You, an artist, should never have created him
In such a dreadful style.
Later on, you'll surely do it better.
But even this distorted caricature can help.
It does not need much altering
For you to see now what it is.
Just notice how the Guardian speaks –
His mournful tone – has too much pathos!
You must not let him speak like this.
And then he'll show you who it is
He's borrowed all this from.

Johannes   Could even the very content of his words
Have been deception?

Double   Don't ask this to Ahriman –
Who always must delight in contradiction.

Johannes   Then who shall I ask?

Double   Just ask yourself.
And I will arm you, richly, with my strength,
So you may find that place in you,
In full wakefulness,
For which no wishes burn,
From where you may truly see.
Make yourself strong!

Johannes   Enchantment that's weaving
Throughout their own being.
Enchantment that's weaving throughout my own being,
Tell me the place – *for which no wishes burn.*

The Guardian disappears. In his place, Benedictus and Maria appear. Ahriman also disappears.

Maria   The image you have of me as well
                 Can only be delusion
                 For the deluding power of wishes
                 Informs your gaze.

Benedictus   And spirit-peacefulness, like a soul-body,
                 Has not yet won mastery of your whole being.

                      The double, Benedictus and Maria disappear.

Johannes (*alone*)
                 Benedictus and Maria, they ... the Guardian!
                 How can they appear before me as the Guardian?

                 Though I have been with you both for many years...
                 It's you I must seek for...
                 This is the strong command
                 Of the enchantment weaving
                 Throughout my own being.

Exit Johannes, stage-right. Strader, Benedictus and Maria enter from the other side.

Strader   When I met you both in spiritual communion
                 At the deep abyss of my own being,
                 You gave, to my inner vision, wise counsel.
                 Though, as yet, I cannot fully understand it,
                 It works on within my soul and will, I know,
                 Unlock for me the answers to those riddles
                 That block me in my further striving.
                 I feel the inner strength that your work gives
                 To pupils on the spirit-path.
                 And so I will be well able to give you all the help you need,
                 To bring about what Hilary has planned,
                 In sacrificial service of mankind.

We have, it's true, to do without Capesius.
The hard work of the others
Will not, of course, replace
The part he played within the whole.
Yet, whatever should happen... will happen.

Benedictus   Whatever should happen, will happen.
These words express the level of your maturity.
They find no echo, though,
In the souls of our other friends.
Johannes is not yet prepared
To bring true spirit-power
Into the world of sense.
And so he too is now withdrawing from the work.
In him, a sign of destiny is shown to us:
We all must seek now for other paths...

Strader   But Maria? [*3rd person*] ... Will *you* not be there, either?

Benedictus   Maria is obliged to bring Johannes with her –
If in truth she is to find the way back
From life in the spirit to the world of sense.
This is what the solemn Guardian wills
Who strictly guards the border where both worlds meet.
For now, she cannot be there at your side.
This should be taken as a clear sign
That at the present time you cannot find
Your way, in truth, into the world of matter.

Strader   So then ... with all my plans... I stand alone.
O solitude – was it you that sought me out,
As I stood at Felix's side?

Benedictus   What has now unfolded within our circle
Has enabled me to read, within the spirit-light,
A word, from the course of your destiny,
Which always had eluded me till now.

I saw you closely joined to types of beings,
Which, if they were creatively involved,
Already now, in human life,
Would bring about evil.
They live, though, in some souls, a seed-like life,
Which will, in future, ripen for the earth.
Such seeds as these I saw within your soul.
That you are not aware of them is for your good.
Through you, they'll first become aware of themselves.
The way that leads into the world of matter
Must stay for now, though, firmly closed to them.

Strader   Whatever else your words might mean,
               They show me solitude will seek me out.
               Solitude itself will have to forge my sword –
               Of which Maria spoke at my abyss.

Benedictus and Maria draw back a little. To Strader, remaining alone, the Soul of Theodora appears.

Theodora's Soul

And Theodora will create warmth for you in realms of light,
So that your spirit-sword may forcefully confront
The opponents of your soul.

She disappears. Exit Strader. Benedictus and Maria step forward.

Maria   My wise teacher, I have never heard you speak
               Words of destiny of such a kind as this
               To pupils at Strader's stage upon the Path.
               Will his soul progress so quickly
               That the power of these words can be healing for him?

Benedictus   Destiny indicated them to me. So it was done.

Maria   And if this power does not prove healing,
               Won't the evil it brings about
               Affect you as well?

Benedictus	It will not bring about evil; And yet I do not know How it will manifest in him. My vision can indeed attain the realms Where counsel such as this lights up in me; But I can see no image of what its effect will be. Each time I try and do this... my seeing dies.
Maria	Your seeing dies? You, my wise teacher? Who is it who can kill your certain spirit-sight?
Benedictus	Johannes – he flees away with it to far-off worlds; We must follow him. I hear him calling.
Maria	He's calling. His call sounds out from wide spirit-spaces. And raying out within it, distant fear.
Benedictus	Thus sounds from endless empty fields of ice, The calling of our friend in far-off worlds.
Maria	The icy cold is *burning* in my being. And fiery flames are kindled deep within me. Flames that swallow up my thinking.
Benedictus	Deep down within you, the fire is blazing That Johannes kindles for himself in cosmic ice and frost.
Maria	The flames are fleeing ... fleeing with my thinking.

And on the distant cosmic shoreline of the soul
A wild battle rages – the battle of my own thinking –
By the stream of nothingness – with cold spirit-light. –
My thinking reels, wavering; – cold light strikes
Hot waves of darkness from my thinking. –
What is it that rises up now from the dark heat? –
It is my own Self in red flames – storming up –
Into the light – the cold light – of the cosmic fields of ice. –

Curtain.

Scene V

The Spiritual World. [The Sun-Sphere.]
   The scene is set in floods of colour: above, reddish going into fiery-red; below, blue going into a dark-blue and violet. At the bottom, a symbolic- seeming earth-sphere.
   The figures appear to blend in with the colours of the whole scene, thus forming together a complete whole. Stage-left – the group of gnomes from Scene 2. In front of them – Hilary. At the very front – the soul-forces. Behind Hilary, somewhat raised – Ahriman. Lucifer at the back – raised and to the left; in the foreground, Felix Balde's Soul. Strader's and Capesius's Souls, Benedictus, Maria, Felicia Balde, The Guardian of the Threshold.

Felix Balde's Soul
(*In the form of a penitent, but wearing a light-violet robe with a gold belt.*)
         I deeply thank you, Spirit who guides these worlds.
         You have released me from the darkness of loneliness.
         Your word awakens all to life and work.
         I shall use what you bestow upon these worlds –
         And when you let my own world sink down into dullness,
         I'll muse upon these worlds.
         You then will bear to them on streaming rays
         What gives to my imagining new power.

Lucifer
(*Bluish-green, shining under-garment; brightly-shining reddish outer-garment in the form of a cloak that extends into wing-like shapes.*
   Above him, instead of an aura, a dark-red headdress in the form of a mitre with wings. On his right wing is a blue, sword-like shape; his left wing supports a yellow, planet-like sphere.)
         My servant, your way of working
         Needs time within the Sun-sphere, which we've entered.
         The earth-star now receives its dullest light.
         This is the time when souls like yours
         Most fruitfully can work upon themselves.

From my great source of light, I let there shine on you
The growing seeds of self-awareness.
Gather them up to make your ego strong.
They'll blossom then in earth-existence –
There your soul will seek these flowers;
And feel delight in its own being,
Passionately musing on its longings.

Felix Balde's Soul (*looking at the group of gnomes*)
There far away a shining life is fading;
In a hazy cloud of images it floats towards the depths;
It wishes, as it floats, to gather weight.

Hilary's Soul
(*Similar in form to a human being, but modified from one of the steel-blue grey elemental beings – the head less bowed and the limbs more human.*)
This hazy cloud of wishes is the Earth Star
Thrown in mirrored image into spirit-realms;
That star for which in this world you fashion
For yourself, out of substances of soul, a thinking life.
To you it's but a hazy passing cloud
But in itself, they're beings, who feel compact of soul.
They labour on the earth with cosmic intellect
In ancient fiery depths which thirst for form.

Felix Balde's Soul
I do not want their weight to be a burden to me.
It stands in opposition to my will to float.

Ahriman
Your words are good! I'll quickly hold them tight –
To keep them for myself unspoiled;
They are not yours to care for any more.
On earth, though, you would hate them.

Strader's Soul
(*Only his head is visible, having a yellow-green aura with red and orange stars. At quite a distance from Felix's Soul.*)
　　　　Words can be heard that sound and then re-echo.
　　　　Words full of meaning, but the sound fades away.
　　　　Desire for life takes hold of the re-echo.
　　　　Which direction will it choose to go in?

The Other Philia
(*Like a copy of Lucifer, but lacking the radiance of his garments. Instead of the sword, a kind of dagger. And instead of the sphere, a red ball like a fruit.*)
　　　　Longing to have weight, it wends its way
　　　　To there where that bright shining life fades away
　　　　And, as a cloud of images, dives into the depths.
　　　　If you can guard, within your realm, that echo's meaning,
　　　　I'll bear its strength for you into that hazy cloud;
　　　　And then you'll find it once again upon the earth.

Philia
(*Angelic form, yellow going into white with bright violet wings, of a lighter shade than those which Maria has later. All three are close to Strader's soul.*)
　　　　I'll take good care for you of that whole cloud of beings,
　　　　So that, unknowingly, they guide your Will;
　　　　Your will I shall entrust unto the cosmic light,
　　　　In which those beings create
　　　　The warmth your being needs.

Astrid
(*Angelic form, light-violet robe with blue wings.*)
　　　　I shall shine out joyfully to those beings
　　　　Radiant starry life, that they condense this
　　　　Into form. For they are far from knowledge, but near
　　　　What stirs the heart. They'll give your earthly body strength.

Luna
(*Slender angelic form, blue-red robe with orange wings.*)
　　　　And I shall hide within your future body

The being of weight they heavily create;
That thinking it, you turn it not to evil
And so unleash a tempest on the earth.

Strader's Soul

All three, they spoke in radiant, sun-filled words.
They work and weave within the sphere around me,
Creating numerous forms and figures.
The urge arises in me, filled with soul-strength,
To meaningfully transform them into one.
Awaken in me, O royal power of the Sun,
That I may dim you down through the resistance
My wishes bring here from the lunar sphere.
A golden glow is rising up already, warming feeling,
And a cold, shimmering light, showering thoughts.
Mercury, ever glimmer, with your passionate life-urges,
Marry together for me the separated being of the world.

I clearly feel: part of that picture
I here am called to work upon, from cosmic spirit-forces,
Has now been recreated for me.

Exit Ahriman.

Capesius's Soul
(*Appearing at Strader's first lines; only his head is visible, which has a blue aura with red and yellow stars.*)

An image rises up, on the far shoreline
Of my soul, that, since wrestling myself free
From earthly life has never touched my being.
It radiates a gentle, healing grace.
The warm and gentle glow of wisdom streams from it;
And it bestows upon me clarifying light.
If I could make this one with me
I would obtain all that for which I thirst.
I do not know the power, though,

> That could make the image
> Come to life within my sphere.

Luna
> What two earth-lives have given you
> You must *feel* –.
> One of them was passed, in ancient times,
> With solemn power of transformation.
> A later life you lived through,
> Greatly darkened by ambition.
> Let the later life be nourished
> By the active powers of grace within the first.
> Then fire-souls from Jupiter will rise and be revealed
> Within the sphere around you.
> You'll know yourself made strong by wisdom.
> That image then, so far away,
> On which you gaze,
> May then move near you.

Capesius's Soul
> To this soul, preparing now for earthly life,
> I must then *owe a debt*,
> So that, within my soul-sphere,
> It reflects itself as *warning-image*?

Astrid
> You do indeed. It is not asking, though,
> To be repaid in your next earthly life.
> The image wants to give you powers of thought
> So you, as man, may recognize the man
> Who in this image shows you
> His future life on earth.

The Other Philia
> The image may indeed draw nearer to you,
> But cannot enter into your own sphere.
> Hold back therefore its longing for your sphere
> That you can find your way again to earth
> Before it flows completely through your being.

Capesius's Soul

> My thankfulness towards this image,
> I feel already, if I can bring
> It near me, and yet, in freedom from it,
> Still remain myself. From Philia's realm
> I now behold, in thought-like images,
> The powers I will gain when it draws near.

Philia

> When soon the light of Saturn, many-coloured,
> Shines upon you – use the hour well!
> The image of the one akin to you in spirit
> Will plant, through Saturn's power, in your soul,
> Deep roots of thinking, which may uncover for you
> The meaningof the course of life on earth,
> When this star carries you once more.

Capesius's Soul

> The counsel that you give will be my guide,
> When Saturn shines upon me.

Lucifer

> Before they earn the right to leave the Sun-sphere,
> Empowered for their later lives on earth,
> I still intend to waken in these souls
> The sight of worlds whose light will cause them pain.
> For sorrow must impregnate them with doubt.
> So I will summon up those spheres of soul
> They do not have the power to look upon.

Benedictus's and Maria's Souls appear in the middle of this domain.
The former as a figure whose dress represents in microcosm the entire visual scene.
Around his head, an aura of red, yellow and blue. The blue blends into the blue-green of his robe, which widens at the bottom.
Maria as an angelic figure – yellow blending into gold, without feet and with light-violet wings.

Benedictus's Soul

> You forcefully impinge upon my world's horizon –
> Your dense spheres so laden with the weight of earth.
> If you allow your sense of self
> To grow too strong,
> My Sunlit being,
> Within this life of Spirit,
> Will not be able to illumine you.

Maria's Soul None of you did know him, last time

> You wore an earthly body;
> But even now there ripens in your souls
> The radiant power of the Sun-filled Word,
> With which in ancient times he nurtured you.
> Feel the deepest impulse in your beings
> And then you will experience him near.

Felix Balde's Soul

> Words resound from spheres I do not know
> But as their tones create no light-filled life
> They are not full reality for me.

Strader's Soul

> A light-filled being is active there, on spirit-shores;
> It is silent for me, though, however hard I try
> And listen to what that light may mean.

Felicia Balde's Soul
(*The figure of a female penitent – yellow-orange robe, silver belt – appearing
near to Maria.*) [*She speaks to Benedictus and Maria.*]

> You souls, summoned here by Lucifer –
> The penitent can hear your words resound,
> But only the Word of the Sun shines out for him;
> Its overpowering brilliance kills your voices.
> The other one beholds your starry light,
> The starry script, though, is unknown to him.

Capesius's Soul

> *The starry script!* – these words awaken thoughts –
> Borne to me on inner tides of soul.
> Thoughts that in a long-past life on earth
> Did wondrously reveal themselves to me.
>
> ------------
>
> They shine out – but fade away the moment they appear;
> Forgetfulness spreads all around its sombre gloom.

Guardian
(*Symbolically represented in the form of an angel, stepping towards and speaking to the souls of Benedictus and Maria.*)

> You two souls, that at Lucifer's command,
> Approached the spheres of these other souls –
> You are, within this place, under my power.
> The souls you seek are seeking you.
> In this cosmic hour, within their spheres,
> None of them, in thought, must touch you
> With their beings. Take heed
> You do not enter in their circle.
> For if you dare to do so,
> It would greatly harm both you and them.
> The starry light that shines in you
> I'd have to weaken
> And banish you from them
> To other realms for long cosmic ages.

Slow curtain.

Scene VI

The Spiritual World, as in the preceding scene. [The Saturn-Sphere.]
The lighting warm and many-shaded, but not too bright. On the left – the
group of sylphs. In front – Philia, Astrid and Luna. Capesius's Soul, Romanus's
Soul, Felix Balde's Soul, then the souls of Torquatus and Bellicosus; the 'Other
Philia' with the souls of Theodora and Felicia Balde.

(Later Benedictus's and Maria's Souls; the Guardian of the Threshold; Lucifer
with Johannes's Soul; finally the Spirit of Johannes's Youth.)

Capesius's Soul

       The image I beheld within the Sun-sphere
       That radiated grace and gentle healing, –
       Works powerfully within me even now,
       When the light of a different wisdom
       Bathes this present spirit-realm
       In shining rays of many colours.
       But now the image works with even greater power.
       It wants me to draw out of it,
       For future earthly ages,
       What the soul inhabiting this image,
       Of such great meaning for my sphere,
       Once gave to me, in a life on earth together.
       And yet, no stream of feeling
       Strongly leads me towards this soul.

Romanus's Soul
(A figure visible from the hips up, with mighty red wings that extend around
his head into a red aura, blending to blue at its rim. Near Capesius's Soul. The
souls of Bellicosus and Torquatus are also nearby.)
       Arouse in you the
       The image of the Jew, who from all sides
       Heard only hate and mockery, and yet
       Gave loyal service to that brotherhood
       To which in former times you once belonged.

Capesius's Soul

   Thought-images now begin to dawn in me,
   Wishing to seize hold of me with all their strength.
   Rising up from welling tides of soul
   The image of *Simon* appears.
   But now there comes towards him – another soul –
   A penitent –
   I'd like to keep him far away from me!

    Felix Balde's Soul appears.

Romanus's Soul

   He can only carry out his work
   At the cosmic hour of Sun;
   When Saturn shines its light upon this realm
   He is a lonely wanderer, shrouded in darkness.

Capesius's Soul

   How this penitent throws me into confusion!
   His soul rays
   Boring deep into my own soul sheaths
   Are burning me.
   Thus it is, when souls behold
   Another's inmost depths.

Felix Balde's Soul (*in a dull, almost veiled voice*)

   'Dear Kean, you have always been a loyal friend...'

Capesius's Soul

   I myself! My own words! Spoken by him –
   Resounding – in echo – in the spirit realm!!
   I must seek this soul.
   He knows me well. Through him I must find myself.

Capesius's Soul disappears. From stage-right the 'Other Philia' and Theodora's Soul appear, followed by Felicia Balde's Soul.

Romanus's Soul

       Over there, two souls approach the penitent.
       Ahead of them that spirit, souls,
       Through love, will always choose to be their guide.
       From one of these two souls there streams
       A gentle light; it flows towards
       The other, who in the image
       Of a penitent woman shows herself.
       This image shines with the glow of beauty,
       Here alive as wisdom.

Torquatus's Soul
(*A figure visible down to the breast, with blue aura and green wings.*)
       You gaze on the reflection of my own heart's longing,
       Which I stream out to you in true spirit-brotherhood.
       For I am given to you, by primal
       Powers of destiny, to waken gentleness.
       Thus do souls serve other souls in spirit.
       On your own, with your rigid mind,
       You'd never find the way to gain
       The living gold of compassion.

Bellicosus's Soul
(*A figure, like Torquatus, visible down to the breast, but with a blue-violet aura and blue-green wings.*)
       Strengthen your spirit-hearing; –
       The soul that shines within that gentle light
       Is speaking. Saturn's light now draws from these souls
       The glory of spirit-blessedness.

Theodora's Soul
(*Angelic form, white with yellow wings and blue-yellow aura.*)
       My true spirit-companion – the burning flames
       Of loneliness threaten to consume the penitent.
       Stream out to him, in gently glowing light,
       Your soul's pure love; this will lessen

Their power and mitigate their heat. –
And guide to him the rays of thought
From all those shadow-beings in motion there. [*The Sylphs.*]
They gather here the forces that they need
To make their soul-like bodies gleam
With glimmering life; so that their quick, creative glimmering
Make strong in human souls on earth
The lively sense for growing and becoming.

Felicia Balde's Soul

You spirit
In the form of a penitent,
Feel my presence.
You sun-filled soul
Receive the strength of the stars. –
Until your spirit-garment
Wrests itself free
From Lucifer's domain –
I shall accompany you, throughout your loneliness,
And bear to you those forces
I will gather for you,
As I make my cosmic way
From star to star.

Theodora's Soul

Previous earthly thoughts arise and glimmer
There on my soul-shore... The image of a human form...
That I did see on earth... has followed here;
It echoes out what once I heard it say:
"Out of the Godhead rose the human soul,
It dies into the depth of being,
Reborn as spirit, it will live again."

During the last speech, Lucifer and Johannes's Soul have appeared.

The Other Philia

> The sounding image bears to you
> The power of noblest brotherly love
> That you unfolded on the earth.
> I shall transform it for you to living power of soul.
> Those shadow beings' [*sylphs*] shimmering light
> Now receives these words of mine.
> Those beings will inspire in you, in earthly life,
> All that they may muse on in eternity. –
> And you, penitent-woman in the land of spirit,
> Guide your steps of soul towards the stars;
> For spirit-daemons long to use your work
> To kindle fantasy in human souls,
> And thus to give their earth-existence wings.

Felicia Balde's Soul

> I'll follow you, dear sister of my soul,
> My Philia, who quickens love,
> From star to star,
> From one spirit to another.
> I'll follow you to starry worlds afar
> And bear your words to many a circling sphere,
> Forming too myself, through all these spirit-workings,
> For my next earthly journey.

Felix Balde's Soul, led by Felicia Balde's Soul, disappears slowly. Theodora remains for a while motionless, gazing at Johannes's Soul; then she too disappears, as does Johannes' soul with Lucifer.

Romanus's Soul [*to Torquatus*]

> That we have seen, within this spirit place
> The word of love and the word of action
> Join in *union* – will give strength
> To seeds within us, that we'll need
> In later lives on earth.

The souls of Romanus, Torquatus and Bellicosus disappear.
The souls of Benedictus and Maria appear beside the Guardian of the Threshold.

Guardian   Recognize your hour of cosmic midnight!
I hold you here beneath the spell of Saturn's ancient,
    ripened light
Until your sheaths,
Illumining yourselves with its light,
Can live its many colours,
With greater power of waking.

Maria's Soul The hour of cosmic midnight with wakefulness of soul? –
The Sun spoke to us, at the time of the Moon
These solemn words of destiny:
"Human souls who live the cosmic midnight hour
In wakefulness, behold how lightnings
Dazzlingly illumine necessities
With such swift flashes that
The spirit-visions die as they're perceived,
And as they die, form
Signs of destiny
That are engraved forever in the soul."
Such souls hear words of thunder
Rolling deep through world-foundations,
And in their rolling threatening
Every soul-delusion.

Lucifer and Johannes's Soul appear again.

Benedictus's Soul
From endless, empty fields of ice
Sounds out the urgent calling of our friend.
If we can recognize the hour of Cosmic Midnight
We'll reach the spirit-circle of his soul.

Maria's Soul The red flames come nearer… with my thinking –
There, from the cosmic shoreline of my soul;

A fiery battle nears; – the battle of my own thinking
With the thoughts of Lucifer;
My own thinking battles in another soul, –
From dark cold is drawn a fiery light.
It flames like lightning! – the fiery light of soul –
The light of soul – in the cosmic fields of ice –.

Lucifer   Recognize this light – my fiery cosmic light, –
And look upon those flashes of lightning,
That your own thinking strikes
From Lucifer's domains of power.
The soul you have so long been bound to
Here I bring into your sphere of vision,
As you experience now the hour of cosmic midnight.
You'll have to seek, though, in a new direction,
Before you may draw truly near this soul.
       [*To Johannes*]
And you – the soul that I have brought here –
Use well the powers of the light
Shining out from Saturn
Into her cosmic midnight hour.

Johannes's Soul
(*Like an angel in form, rose-red, without feet and with blue-red wings.*)
I feel the presence of souls, but lack the power
So to strengthen their light in me
That it become real being.
However *near* they may be,
Only in the far distance
Do I see their thinking shine.
How can I raise them up into my spirit-sight?

Philia   You will behold them
If you can quickly grasp
What they themselves illumine
In the cosmic light.

But when you see them –
Use the moment's flash;
For what will be illumined
Will swiftly fade away.

Johannes's Soul

The words the teacher's speaking to his pupil –
The pupil, who's so near to me in soul –
Shall now illumine my own soul-sphere.

Benedictus's Soul

At this spirit-midnight-hour
Bring forth the powers of Will
You then will want to feel again,
When earthly strength
Flows through your form.
Your words, they will illumine your friend's soul.

Maria's Soul Then let my words grow strong,
That I, at cosmic midnight,
Offer to the soul that Lucifer has brought me.
What is most dear to me in depths of soul
I shall behold and let it sound,
So that it form into a tone,
A tone his soul on earth may feel,
And lovingly let live within his being.
What is it I behold in depths of soul?
I see shine out a sacred, fiery script.
A noble, fiery script is shining there.
Love for the soul of my teacher flames out.
He, who on earth and in the spirit,
Has accompanied me through long ages;
Who, when my ardent prayer sought him
At times of danger, always found me,
Even when he dwelt in heights of spirit;
Radiantly bright this love appears to me –

Let this Word of Love sound out from me to that other soul. –

But now…
What flames are these, the Word of Love awakens?
They shine so gently – and from their gentleness
Streams a deep solemnity;
Wisdom's lightning flashes through the ether,
Bestowing grace. And blessedness,
Pouring forth, joyfully weaves
Through all the wide horizons of my soul.
Everlasting Time – I do entreat you –
Pour yourself out into this blessedness,
And together with me,
Let the teacher, and the other soul as well,
Linger now within you, full of peace.

Guardian   Then let the lightning flashes fade now into nothingness –
Flashes that dazzlingly illumine necessities
When wakeful souls experience World-North.
Let the deep-resounding thunder, rolling
With warning at the hour of cosmic midnight,
Also now grow quiet. And now, to you,
Astrid, a strict command is given.
Safely guard this tempest of the soul
Until her next cosmic midnight finds her soul
Awakening in the stream of time.
She then will have to stand
Quite differently before herself, – –
She'll see an image of herself from ancient times,
And come to know
How even in the falling of the soul
Its wings gain greater strength
For the ascent to spirit-heights.
The soul must *never wish to fall*;
But every time it falls must gain new wisdom.

Astrid   The thunder and the lightning's power
          I'll safely hold,
          And thus they may be kept in world-existence,
          Till Saturn once again turns to her soul.

Maria's Soul Abiding here, I feel the blessedness of stars,
          Which I'm allowed to enter
          In the stream of time.
          Carried by its grace,
          I'll live a life creating
          Together with the soul
          So closely bound to mine.

Luna   I'll guard all your creating
          Here in spirit
          So that its fruits
          Shall ripen for you
          On the earth.

Johannes's Soul
          Into the sphere of my soul – this star!
          It shines with blessing – rays out grace –
          A soul-star – floating – through the ether –
          But there – in the dull light – another star –
          Sounding quietly; but I wish to hear it.

*With these last words, the Spirit of Johannes's Youth appears – like an angel with
a silvery light.*

Spirit of Johannes's Youth
          I feed with my life your wishes and desires;
          When worlds lure you,
          Into which I may joyfully lead you,
          My breath will shine strength
          Into your youthful goals.
          But when you lose me in yourself,
          Then, a being without being,

I must offer up my life to the shades.
Blossom of my life – do not abandon me.

Lucifer   He will not abandon you – I see desires
For light within his being's depths
Which cannot follow in the footsteps of the other soul. –
When these desires, with all the glory they give rise to,
Take root as Being deep within his soul,
He will not wish to see their precious fruits
Be squandered in that realm
Where Love alone holds sway, without Beauty.

Slow curtain.

Scene VII

A temple in a somewhat Egyptian style – a place of initiation in the third cultural epoch of the earth. On stage – the Hierophant (of the Sacrifice), the Threshold Guardian and the Mystic.

(In this and in the following scene, the name of the individuality in his or her modern incarnation is given on their first appearance – RR.)

Hierophant (*Capesius*)
> Has everything been worthily prepared,
> > my Threshold Guardian,
> In order that our holy rite may be of service
> Both to humankind and the gods?

Threshold Guardian (*Felix*)
> As far as human beings can foresee,
> All has been well prepared; the space of the Temple
> Has been filled for many days with sacred incense.

Hierophant My Mystic, the priest who undergoes these rites today,
> To whom the hallowed secrets of wisdom will be revealed,
> Will become the counsellor to the King.
> Did you structure his trials in such a way
> That he does not solely devote himself
> To a spirit-wisdom that has no care for earthly life?
> For such a counsellor would be damaging for us.

Mystic (*Felicia*)
> His trials were carried out correctly,
> And the Masters have approved of them.
> It seems to me, however, that this Mystic
> Has little care for earthly matters;
> His soul is entirely focussed
> On spirit-striving and his own development.
> He could well be seen
> As enraptured by the spirit.

It would not be too much to say
That he positively indulges himself
In the feeling of being wholly at one
With the spirit.

Hierophant   Have you often seen him in such a state?

Mystic   Yes. He really does appear like this quite frequently.
              He surely would be better suited
              To serve in the inner Temple,
              Rather than as your Counsellor.

Hierophant   (That's) Enough. Return to your duties.
             And see to it that our sacred rite
             Is carried out correctly.

                    Exit Mystic.

             But with you, my Threshold Guardian,
             I must speak further.
             I greatly value, as you know, your mystic gifts.
             For me you stand much higher with your wisdom
             Than your role within the Temple indicates –
             And I have often checked my own spirit-sight
             Against what you are able to see.
             So tell me: how great is your trust
             In the neophyte's spiritual maturity?

Threshold Guardian
             Who wants to hear my view?
             My voice is never considered.

Hierophant   I always consider it.
             Today once again you will stand at my side.
             We must follow this sacred rite with exact
             Soul-vision; and if what the neophyte experiences in spirit
             Is in the slightest way unfitting to the high purposes of this ritual
             I shall prevent him becoming a counsellor.

Threshold Guardian
>What is it within the neophyte
>That the ritual might reveal?

Hierophant I know he does not merit the high honour
>Which those who serve the temple
>Seek to confer on him.
>I know his human nature well.
>For him, mysticism is not
>What wakens in the human heart
>When, from above,
>The grace-filled light of spirit
>Draws souls unto itself.
>Passions surge through his being.
>The clamorous urges of the senses have not yet grown
>>silent for him.
>Of course I do not wish to counter the Will of the Gods,
>Which, in world-becoming,
>Even shines its wise light
>Through passion and the senses' urges.
>But when such urges hide themselves
>Behind a mask of mystical devotion
>It only leads to self-deception
>And to an impure Will.
>Into such souls the light that weaves as being
>Through spirit-worlds cannot enter.
>Passion darkens it to a mystic fog.

Threshold Guardian
>My hierophant, you pass strict judgement
>On one who is young and inexperienced,
>So cannot know himself.
>All he can do is follow
>What the leaders of the Temple
>Describe as the correct soul-path.

Hierophant I do not wish to pass judgement on the man
           But only on the *deed*
           That will occur
           Within this solemn, holy place.
           The sacrificial work that we perform
           Is not just of significance here;
           Events of world-destiny
           Stream through all the words and deeds
           Of these most sacred rites.
           What here takes place in image-form
           Has ever-active power of being in spirit-worlds.
           But now, my threshold-guardian – to your work.
           You will yourself discover
           How you best may help me
           During the ritual.

                    Exit Threshold Guardian.

Hierophant (*alone*)
           It will not be the fault of this young Mystic,
           Who offers himself today to Wisdom,
           If in the next few hours feelings that have no place here,
           But might well stream from his heart,
           Shine out into our sacrificial rite –
           Feelings that, within the image of this ritual,
           Would mystically rise up into spirit-spheres,
           From where destructive forces, later,
           Would then flow back into earthly life –
           It will be those who lead and guide these rites
           Who will be guilty.
           Do even they – I have to ask – still recognize the Mystic Power
           That spiritually pours through
           Every Word and every Sign
           Within this place – that never ceases *working*,
           Even if soul-substance
           Pours into these Words and Signs

That is not beneficial
To the development of the world?
For rather than this young Mystic
Offering himself, consciously, to the Spirit,
He is dragged by his teachers,
As a sacrifice,
To the place of initiation;
Where, in unconsciousness,
He will commit to the spirit
His life of soul,
Which, if he could live it out consciously, *within* himself,
He would in fact direct along other paths.
Within the community of our Mystic Priests
Only the Highest Hierophant of the Sacred Rite
Is fully aware
Of what lives, as hidden power,
Within the forms of the ritual.
But he is as silent as solitude itself;
As his inner nobility
Strictly commands.
The others gaze
With blank incomprehension
When I try and talk
About the earnestness of the ritual.

Thus I am completely alone with my concerns –
Which, when I sense the profundity of this place of sacrifice –
So often weigh me down within.
I certainly have come to know here deeply:
Solitude – at the most solemn site of the spirit.
Why am I alone within this place?
The soul cannot but ask this; – but when will the Spirit
Give *this soul* an answer!

Slow curtain.

Scene VIII

The same temple setting as in scene 7; at first it is covered by an intermediate curtain, in front of which an Egyptian woman speaks the following. The Egyptian woman is to be thought of as a previous incarnation of Johannes Thomasius.

Egyptian Woman (*Johannes*)

> In this very hour he is offering himself up
> In service of the age-old, holy Mysteries, –
> And must tear himself away from me for ever.
> From those same light-filled heights,
> To which *his* soul now turns,
> Must *mine* receive the ray of death; – for without him –
> All I can hope to find on earth is
> Sorrow, loss, suffering – and death – –.
>
> ------------
>
> Even if he is leaving me, though,
> I will remain very near this place
> Where he gives himself in trust to the spirit.
> Even if I am not permitted to see with my eyes
> How he wins his way free from the earth –,
> Through some revelation
> While dreaming
> Perhaps I may still now
> Linger with him
> A while
> In the spirit.

The curtain opens revealing everything made ready for the initiation of the Neophyte, who is to be thought of as an earlier incarnation of Maria; on one side of the sacrificial altar stands the Highest Hierophant, who is to be thought of as an earlier incarnation of Benedictus; on the other side of the Altar, the Keeper of the Word, an earlier incarnation of Hilary; somewhat in front of the altar, the Keeper of the Seals, an earlier incarnation of Theodora; then on one side of the altar towards the front: The Representative of the Earth Element, an earlier incarnation of Romanus; the Representative of the Air Element, an earlier incarnation of Magnus Bellicosus; very close to the Highest Hierophant stands the Hierophant, an earlier incarnation of Capesius; on the other side: the Representative of the Fire Element, an earlier incarnation of Dr. Strader; the Representative of the Water Element, an earlier incarnation of Torquatus. In front: Philia, Astrid, Luna and the 'Other Philia'. At the very front in the form of the Sphinxes – Lucifer and Ahriman; Lucifer in such a way that the Angel (the Cherub) is more emphasized, Ahriman in such a way that the Bull is more emphasized.

Four other priests stand at the front.

After the Temple hall has become visible, there is a soundless stillness. Then the Neophyte is led in through the gates on the left by the Threshold Guardian, an earlier incarnation of Felix Balde, and the Mystic, an earlier incarnation of Felicia Balde. They postion him in the inner circle close to the altar. They both remain standing near him.

The Threshold Guardian (*Felix*)
> The Mystic has brought you here
> From that woven web of semblance
> That you, in the darkness of your error,
> Did name 'the world'.
> From being and from nothingness
> Was the world woven,
> Which for you did weave itself
> Into a semblance.
> Semblance is good, when beheld
> In the light of Being.
> But you have but dreamed it
> In your life of semblance.
> And semblance
> Known only by semblance
> Falls from the wholeness of the world.
> You semblance of a semblance –
> Learn to know yourself!

The Mystic (*Felicia*)
> Thus speaks the one,
> Who guards the threshold of this temple.
> Experience in yourself
> The heavy weight of his word.

The Representative of the Element of Earth (*Romanus*)
> In the heavy weight of Earth-existence
> Grasp, without fear, the semblance of who you are,
> That you may sink into the depths of the world –
> There in the darkness, seek for being;
> Unite what you may find with your own semblance;
> In ever weighing down it will grant you being.

The Keeper of the Word (*The Recorder*) (*Hilary*)
> Sinking down into the depths
> You will not understand
> Where we are leading you
> Until you have obeyed his word.
> Here we forge your being's very form;
> Recognize our work, for otherwise,
> You would dissolve completely
> As a semblance,
> In universal nothingness.

The Mystic   Thus speaks the one
> Who guards the words of this temple.
> Experience in yourself
> What lives within the words
> As down-bearing weight.

The Representative of the Element of Air (*Magnus Bellicosus*)
> Flee the heavy weight of earth existence;
> In making you sink down
> It kills your selfhood's being.
> With lightness of the air fly fast away. –
> In the world's wide distances, in shining light,

Seek for being.
Unite what you find with your own semblance;
In high uplifting flight it will grant you being.

The Keeper of the Word
    Rising up in flight
    You will not understand
    Where we are leading you
    Until you have obeyed his word.
    We shine into your being's very life;
    Recognize our work; for otherwise
    You would dissolve completely
    As a semblance,
    In universal weight.

The Mystic Thus speaks the one
    Who guards the words of this temple.
    Experience in yourself
    What lives within his words
    As wingéd power of flight.

The Highest Hierophant (Benedictus)
    My son, upon the noble paths of wisdom,
    You rightly will obey these mystics' words.
    Within yourself you cannot see the answer.
    For darkness of error still does weigh you down.
    And foolishness within you strives for distant worlds.
    Gaze therefore – into this flame –

(*Upon the altar, standing in the middle, the sacred fire flares up in bright and leaping tongues of flame*)

    Which is much nearer to you
    Than the life of your own being.
    And read within the fire your answer.

The Mystic Thus speaks the one
    Who leads the sacrificial rites of this temple.

Experience in yourself
The hallowed, consecrating power
Within these rites.

The Representative of the Element of Fire (*Strader*)
Let the error of your sense of self
Be *burned up* within the fire,
Lit for you within this sacrifice.
Burn up *yourself* – with all the substance of your error. –
Within the cosmic fire now seek your being as flame –
Unite what you find with your own semblance.
In fierily burning it will grant you being.

The Guardian of the Seals (*Theodora*)
Burning,
You will not understand
Why we now forge you into flame,
Until you have obeyed his word.
We purify your being's very form. –
Recognize our work, for otherwise
You'll lose yourself, in formlessness, amidst the cosmic Water.

The Mystic   Thus speaks the one
Who guards the seal of this temple.
Experience in yourself
The radiant, light-filled power of wisdom.

The Representative of the Element of Water (*Torquatus*)
The flaming power within the worlds of fire
Withstand – for it would sap the strength of your own being.
The only way – for you – that semblance may arise to being
Is if the lapping, beating waves of cosmic water
Can fill you with the echoing tones that sound throughout
   the spheres.
In cosmic water, as a wave, now seek for being.
Unite what you find with your own semblance.
In flowing and in surging it will grant you being.

The Guardian of the Seals
>Surging,
>You will not understand
>Why we now mould you as a wave
>Until you have obeyed his word.
>We mould your very being's form.
>Recognize our work, for otherwise
>You'll lose yourself, in formlessness, within the cosmic fire.

The Highest Hierophant
>My son, employing all your powers of will,
>You also will obey *these* mystics' words.
>Within yourself you cannot see the answer.
>In coward fear your power freezes still.
>You are too weak to form yourself as wave,
>That could ring out amidst the sounding spheres.
>So hear then now the forces of your soul;
>And recognize they speak with your own voice.

Philia
>In fire purify yourself – as cosmic wave
>Then lose yourself
>Amidst the tones of spirit-spheres.

Astrid
>Amidst the tones of spirit-spheres now form yourself; –
>Take flight, with all the lightness of the air,
>To distant worlds.

Luna
>In cosmic depths sink down with weight of earth;
>And in the heavy weight
>Take courage – as yourself.

The Other Philia
>Leave far behind all trace of your own being;
>Unite yourself with all the powers that live and move
>Throughout the elemental world.

The Mystic Thus speaks within the Temple *your own* soul,
>Experience in it now the guiding power of its forces.

The Highest Hierophant
> You, my companion – Hierophant –
> *Fathom* in its very depths
> This soul we are to lead onto the path of wisdom –
> Proclaim to us your vision
> Of its present state.

The Hierophant (*Capesius*)
> All that our rites should bring about has happened.
> The soul has now forgotten what it was.
> The contradictory powers within the elements have quite erased
> Its woven web of semblance, spun by error;
> This lives on now in elemental strife.
> The soul has only saved its being.
> What lives within its being it must read
> Within the cosmic Word
> That speaks from out the fiery flame.

Highest Hierophant
> Then read to us, you human soul, what the flame
> Proclaims to you as cosmic word
> Within your inmost being.

----

*There is a long pause, during which it becomes completely dark – only the flame
and the indefinite outlines of the people can be seen. The Highest Hierophant
then continues.*

> From out your cosmic vision now awake!
> Proclaim what in the World-Word can be read –

The Neophyte says nothing. The Highest Hierophant continues with alarm.

> Nothing! – Is it gone? Your vision? – Speak!

The Neophyte (*Maria*)
> Obeying your strict and sacrificial Word,
> I wholly sank into the being of the flame,
> Expecting sounds of high, exalted Cosmic Words.

(The mystics present, with the exception of the Hierophant, show an ever-increasing horror during the speech of the Neophyte.)

I then began to feel how I, light as air,
Could free myself from earthly weight. – –
So lovingly received by cosmic fire
I felt myself in ever-flowing streams of spirit-waves.
I saw, how as another being,
My earthly form remained, outside myself. –
Though wholly wrapped around with bliss,
Feeling myself within the spirit-light,
I could not help but look upon the earthly covering there
With sympathy and feelings full of longing.
Spirits from the higher worlds
Rayed down their light upon it.
And then, like butterflies, glittering and bright,
There suddenly drew near
The lively beings who cared and tended for its life.
The shimmering light of these beings
Was reflected by the body
In a dazzling display of colours
That first shone gloriously near,
Then glimmered far away
Then finally, scattering,
Was lost in space.
And then, within my spirit-soul existence,
The wish sprang up in me
That weight of earth
Might sink me down
Into my body's covering
So I might let the feeling grow
Of joy in life's warmth. –
Happily plunging down into my body,
I heard your strict loud summons to awake.

The Highest Hierophant (*speaking with alarm to the alarmed mystics*)
      This is not spirit-vision; – but earthly feeling –
      It freed itself from the mystic – and rose up
      Into the light-filled spirit-heights
      As sacrifice.
      O sacrilege!
      Sacrilege – – !

The Keeper of the Word (*furiously, to the Hierophant*)
      This could never have been possible
      Had you performed
      According to all its ancient sacred duties
      Your office as hierophant.

The Hierophant
      I did what in this sacrificial hour
      Was laid upon me
      As duty
      From higher realms.
      I did
      Hold back
      From thinking on the words
      That I am bidden to, by custom,
      Which from my thinking
      Then should spiritually have passed across
      To the neophyte.
      The young man
      Has not proclaimed, therefore,
      The thinking of another –
      He has proclaimed here
      His own being.
      Truth has conquered. ---
      You may well punish me;
      I had to do
      What you experienced with so much fear.
      I feel the times approach already

Which will set free
The individual I
From out the spirit of the group
And grant it thinking of its own.
The youth may now perhaps escape
Your Mystic Path –.
But later lives on earth
Will show to him without doubt the mystic ways
That have been foreordained for him by destiny.

The Mystics [*first in individual voices and small groups – RR*]
        O sacrilege!
        It cries out for atonement –
        For punishment –
        The deed must be atoned –
        Yes – punishment!
        He has to pay the price!
        It is an outrage to the gods.
In Chorus: O Sacrilege!!!

The sphinxes, that were immobile as statues, begin to speak – as Ahriman and Lucifer. The Hierophant, the Highest Hierophant and the Neophyte are the only ones to hear them; – the others remain in a state of great agitation because of what has happened.

Ahriman as Sphinx
        I have to seize and capture for my realm
        What here, unjustly, wills to come to light.
        I then will have to foster it in darkness.
        And thus, in spirit, it should form the power
        In future times, befitting world-evolving,
        To interweave itself in human life,
        In ways that rightly benefit mankind.
        But till it has obtained this power, then *all*
        That here has proved itself an earthly burden on
        This sacrificial rite will serve *my* work.

Lucifer as Sphinx
> I will lead away to my domain
> What here, as spirit-wishing, joys in semblance.
> As semblance, it will radiantly shine
> Within the light, and thus in spirit-realms
> Will wholly consecrate itself to Beauty.
> To Beauty, which the burden of the weight
> Of earth still keeps from him in present times –
> In Beauty semblance turns itself to Being –
> In future it will be the Light of Earth;
> As light descending, which now flees from here.

The Highest Hierophant
> The sphinxes speak, –
> They, who ever since these rites were first performed here –
> Have been but image.
> The spirit – it has taken hold of lifeless form.
> O destiny – you sound out as Word of Worlds.

The other mystics, except for the Hierophant and the Neophyte, are astonished by the words of the Highest Hierophant.

The Hierophant (*to the Highest Hierophant*)
> The sacrificial work that we perform
> Is not just of significance here;
> Events of world-destiny
> Stream through all the words and deeds
> Of these most sacred rites.

Over the mood created by all that has happened, the curtain falls.

Scene IX

A small room – like a study – with a serious mood – in Hilary's house. At first, Maria – alone in meditation – (then there appear: Astrid, Luna, The Guardian of the Threshold and Benedictus.)

Maria   There – upon the shoreline of the spirit – a soul-star, –
Coming near, – radiant in spirit – drawing near me –
Draws near to me – with my own self, – and nearing –
Its light grows ever stronger – and more peaceful.
O star that has appeared within my spirit-sphere,
What is it that your nearing shines
Into the inner seeing of my soul?

Astrid appears.

Astrid   Recognize what I may now bestow on you;
for from the battle of the light
With darknesses
I wrested free your thinking's power;
And from the mighty moment of awakening
Within the cosmic midnight hour
I now do faithfully bring it back
Into your earthly form.

Maria   You, my Astrid, you always have appeared till now,
But as a shining shadow of the soul;
What is it that transforms you
Into a bright spirit-star?

Astrid   The thunder and the lightning's power I kept for you,
And thus it was held safe for you in world-existence –
And now you may behold it knowingly
Remembering the hour of cosmic midnight.

Maria   The hour of cosmic midnight!
Before the body's covering
For this life on earth

Enclosed my Self –
Through which I stayed awake
Amidst the richly coloured light of Saturn!
Till now my earthly thinking
Covered this experience in spirit
In dimness of the soul; –
It rises now to full-lit clarity of soul within me.

Astrid   Within the cosmic light you spoke these words yourself:
"Everlasting time – I do entreat you –
Pour yourself into this blessedness,
And together with me,
Let the teacher and the other soul aswell
Linger now within you, full of peace."

Maria   May you also linger for me
You – this present moment – now –
Who found the way
To fashion into strength of self
This happening in the spirit. Arm my soul,
So that you do not vanish like a dream.
Within the light illumining the hour of Cosmic Midnight,
Which Astrid makes to shine from dimness of the soul,
My I unites itself unto that I
That did create me
So that I could be of service to it
Within the being of the world.
But how may I keep hold of you
You present moment,
So I don't lose you
When the senses feel once more
The brightness of the earth around me?
For the senses' power is very great;
And if they kill what has been seen in spirit
Very often this cannot revive
When one refinds oneself again in spirit.

On the last words, as if called up by them, Luna appears.

Luna   Before the world of sense-existence
Leads you once again to dreaming
Safely guard your strength of will
Which could create this moment for you.
Recall the words I spoke
When at the hour of Cosmic Midnight
You beheld me.

Maria   My Luna, you have brought me here,
From Cosmic Midnight,
The *strength of will*
Which shall uphold me
In my earth-existence.

Luna   My words were followed by the Guardian's warning:
"You now will have to stand
Quite differently before yourself;
You'll see an image of yourself from ancient times
And come to know
How even in the *falling* of the soul
Its wings gain greater strength
For the ascent to spirit-heights.
The soul must *never wish to fall*;
But every time it falls must gain new wisdom."

- - - - - - - - - - -

Maria   The power of your words
Carries me away.
Where is it taking me?
There – upon the shoreline of my soul – a spirit-star! –
It's shining – drawing near – as spirit-form;
Draws near to me – with my own self, – and nearing
Its light condenses – more and more. – Forms
Within the light are growing darker –
Reveal themselves as living beings – !
A young neophyte, a sacrificial flame,

The highest hierophant's
Most strict command
To rightly read and to make known
The content of the flame!

The horror and complete confusion of the Mystics,
At that young Mystic's declaration
About himself!

The Guardian of the Threshold appears during these last words.

Guardian   In spirit-hearing too
Fathom for yourself once more
The highest hierophant's
Most strict command.

Maria   "Then read to us, you human soul, what the flame
proclaims to you
As cosmic word within your inmost being."
Who spoke this Word that my own thinking
Bears to me, remembering,
From flowing tides of soul?

Benedictus appears during Maria's words.

Benedictus You call me here to you with my own words.
When with these words, in ages past, I once commanded you,
They did not find you ready yet to follow me.
They *rested* – deeply held
Within the happening of the world;
In lengthy course of time they gathered strength
That flowed towards them from your life of soul.
And thus they worked, unconsciously, in you,
In deepest soul-foundations,
Within your later lives on earth –
And let you find me, once again, as teacher.
They *now* transform themselves within you, consciously,
through thinking,

To living strength-filled content for your life:
"The sacrificial work that we perform
Is not just of significance here;
Events of world-destiny
Stream through all the words and deeds
Of these most sacred rites."

Maria   It was not *you* who spoke those words.
It was the hierophant, he who in
That ancient temple brotherhood
Was your companion.
That powers of destiny
Had already foreseen
The ending of that Brotherhood
Was known to him. –
He beheld, unconsciously,
The beautiful appearance of the dawn
That heralded already, over Greece,
A new Sun rising
In the spiritual stream of Earth.
And therefore he suppressed the thoughts
That he should have directed to my soul.
He made himself an instrument of the Cosmic Spirit
At that initiation and sacred rite,
Through which he heard the evolving stream of world-events
Whispering within him.
He spoke these words as well, from inmost depths of soul:
"I certainly have come to know here deeply:
Solitude – at the most solemn site of the spirit.
Why am I alone within this place?"

Benedictus   Thus there sprang up in his soul the urge
For *solitude*; in the womb of time
This seed within his soul has ripened into fruit.
Capesius – as a Mystic – now experiences this fruit;
And this it is that makes him wish to follow
Felix's example.

Maria   But that woman,
             Who stayed so near the Temple;
             I see her well in ancient time –
             My vision, though, cannot yet reach her
             In her present form; how may I find her
             When sense-existence leads me once again
             To dreaming?

The Guardian
             When you behold the being, within the realm of soul,
             That he can feel as shadow among shadows
             Then you will find her.
             She seeks this being with all her strength of soul.
             She will only redeem it from the realm of shades
             When in her present form, through you,
             She can behold her long-past life on earth.

The Guardian of the Threshold and Benedictus disappear.

Maria   The solemn Guardian glides away, as shining soul-star,
             Towards the shoreline of my soul – ;
             A holy power sublime rays forth from him; –
             His great solemnity
             Pours strength throughout my deepest being;
             I will immerse myself within this peace – – ;
             I feel already how, through this,
             I'll lead myself to full awakening in the spirit.
             And you, my messengers of soul – –
             I'll keep alive within my being
             As stars that light the way – – .
             On you, Astrid, will I call, when thoughts
             Would separate from soul's true brightness.
             And you, O Luna, may my Word then always find you
             When power of will is sleeping in soul-depths.

Curtain while Maria, Astrid and Luna are still in the room.

Scene X

The same room as in scene nine. At first, Johannes alone, in meditation. (Later there appear: the 'Other Philia', Maria, the Spirit of Johannes's Youth, Lucifer, Benedictus.)

Johannes "In this very hour he is offering himself up
In service of the age-old, holy Mysteries – ;
Through some revelation
While dreaming
Perhaps I may still now
Linger with him
A while
In the spirit."
This was how, in times long past, quite near the Temple,
The woman spoke, whom I behold in spirit-image,
And thinking of her, I feel new strength is given to me.
What does this image do to me? What is it
That transfixes me, almost spellbound, when I see it?
It's certainly not interest, that from the very image itself
Forces itself on me; for should this image
Appear before me in sense-existence,
It would seem quite meaningless.
What is it that from this image
Speaks to me?

The Other Philia
Enchantment that's weaving
Throughout their own being.

Johannes For now waking dreaming
To souls is revealing
Enchantment that's weaving
Throughout their own being.

While Johannes is speaking these words, the 'Other Philia' comes towards him.

Who are you, mysterious and magical spirit?
You brought my soul your good and true advice
And yet, about *yourself*, you all the time deceived me.

The Other Philia

It's you who have created, from yourself,
This double form of your being.
Like a shade, I too am forced to hover round you
Till you yourself redeem *that shade*
Given, by your guilt, a trapped, enchanted life.

Johannes   For the third time – you speak these words
Which I will follow. – Show me how to do so.

The Other Philia

Seek for what has been preserved within yourself, Johannes,
That goes on living in the spirit-light.
It will give light to you from its own light.
And then you will be able to behold, within you,
How in your future life
You may erase your guilt.

Johannes   How can I seek for what has been preserved within myself,
That goes on living in the spirit light?

The Other Philia

Give me all you are yourself in thinking;
Only for a little while, lose yourself in me;
Do it, though, in such a way, that you do *not* become another.

Johannes   How can I give myself to you
Before I have been able to behold you
In your true being?

The Other Philia

I am within you – part of your own soul.
The power of love itself – am I in you;
The hope that fills the heart, that stirs in you,

The fruits of long-past lives on earth, that have
Been kept for you, within your being – O
Behold these now through me – my presence feel –
And through my strength in you, behold yourself.
Unveil within yourself the being in that image
Created without interest by your vision.

The 'Other Philia' disappears.

Johannes   O mysterious spirit –
I feel your presence within me –
Yet cannot see you any more.
Where is it
That you live for me?

The 'Other Philia' calls, as if from far away.

The Other Philia
Enchantment that's weaving
Throughout their own being.

Johannes   Enchantment that's weaving
Throughout their own being.
Enchantment that's weaving throughout *my* own being,
Unveil for me the being in that image
Created without interest by my vision.

The power of these words
Carries me away.
Where is it taking me?
There upon the shoreline of the soul – a spirit-star!
It's shining, drawing near – as spirit-form,
And as it nears, growing brighter; – figures take on form; –
And now begin to live and move like beings; –
A young neophyte, – a sacrificial flame,
The highest hierophant's
Most strict command

To rightly read and to make known
The content of the flame. –

The woman – (the image created without interest by my vision) –
Is searching for the young neophyte.

Maria appears as a thought-form of Johannes.

Maria   Who thought of you before the sacrificial flame?
          Who felt you there so near the sacred place?

Johannes, if you would free your spirit-shadow
From worlds of soul where it's enchanted,
Then you must *live* the goals
That strive from it towards you;
The trail that you are following – it will guide you;
But first you have to rightly find it once again.
The woman standing near the temple,
When she is living strongly in your thoughts,
Will show it to you.
Enchanted in the realm of shadow-spirits,
She strives towards that other shadow,
Who now, through you, must serve cruel shades,
And do their dreadful work.

The Spirit of Johannes's Youth appears.

The Spirit of Johannes's Youth
          I will be always bound to you in future
          If you will nurture lovingly those powers
          Which in the womb of time were kept for me
          So faithfully by that young neophyte
          For whom your soul once searched within the Temple.
          But you must also see the spirit truly
          By whose side I now appear to you.

| Maria | Maria, as you wish to see her, |
| | Does not exist in worlds where truth prevails. |

Maria, as you wish to see her,
Does not exist in worlds where truth prevails.
My solemn holy vow rays out its strength,
Which shall preserve for you what you've achieved.
You find me in the glorious fields of light
Where radiant beauty brings to birth the powers of life;
Seek for me in depths of worlds,
Where souls are willing to attain the feeling of the gods,
Through Love, which always sees the Self within the All.

Lucifer appears, while Maria is speaking the last line.

Lucifer   Then work, compelling powers
And elemental spirits, feel
The power of your master.
Make straight the path
Along which can be led
Away from bounds of earth
Into bright Lucifer's domain
All that my wishes crave
And that must be obedient to my will.

Benedictus appears.

Benedictus Maria's holy solemn vow now works
And pours into his soul its healing radiance.
He will admire you,
But will *not* succumb to you.

Lucifer   Then I will fight.

Benedictus And fighting serve the gods!

Curtain.

Scene XI

The same room as in the two previous scenes.
Benedictus and Strader enter the room.

Strader. You spoke serious words to me
And Maria very harsh ones
When you both showed yourselves to me
At my life's abyss.

Benedictus The images, you know, are not essential;
But the content,
That wishes to get through to the soul
And to reveal itself within the image.

Strader Yet what spoke from these images was harsh:
"Where is your light? You radiate darkness,
You're creating wild, confusing darkness in the light."
The spirit – in Maria's image – really spoke like this.

Benedictus As you have climbed up one step higher,
On the spiritual path,
The spirit who has led you up, towards itself,
Revealed what you have previously achieved
As darkness.
That spirit chose Maria's image
For this was how your own soul pictured it.
My dear Strader,
Powerfully the spirit
Now holds sway within you –
It leads you on
In swift-winged flight
To ever higher stages of your soul.

Strader And yet the words ring out quite dreadfully within me:
"Because you are too cowardly to radiate your light."
The Spirit in that image said this too.

Benedictus   The Spirit had to name you cowardly,
As what for lesser souls is bravery
For yours indeed is only cowardice.
As we develop, what was once courageous
Turns to cowardice
That must be overcome.

Strader   Your words... they touch me deeply!
Romanus spoke with me, a while ago,
About his plan.
I should, he said, no longer carry out the project
In unity with you, but on my own, without your help.
And he would then commit himself to stand by Hilary,
With everything he owns. –
When I objected, saying I would never
Contemplate the work
In separation from your circle
He declared that in that case
All further efforts were in vain.
Romanus now supports the opposition
Hilary's manager is putting up against
The project, without which my life, indeed,
Must seem completely worthless.
As these two men now rob from me
My very field of action, I see before me
Nothing – other than a life that lacks
The very air we need to live.
So that my spirit is not
Lamed now, in its flight,
I need that courage
You just spoke about.
Though whether I will prove strong enough for this,
I cannot say,
For I can feel
How that same power I'm seeking to unchain

Is also turning now, destructively,
Against me.

Benedictus   Maria and Johannes have recently
Progressed in spiritual vision.
What hindered them before,
From stepping from the Mystic Life
Into the world of sense-existence,
Is gone; in the further course of time
There will be found new goals
Which will bring you and them together.
The Mystic Words do not just guide
They do themselves create new forces –
Whatever must happen… will happen.
We therefore will await, in watchfulness,
To see the way the spirit shows its signs.

Strader   What I can only see to be a sign of destiny
Formed recently for me into an image.
I was on a ship; *you* were at the helm;
I had to make the ship go.
We were taking Maria and Johannes
To where they could start their work;
There then appeared, very near to us,
Another ship; in it was Romanus
And Hilary's friend, the Manager.
They blocked our path, confronting us as enemies.
I started battling against them – but suddenly
Into the battle stepped Ahriman,
Fighting on their side.
I saw myself in bitter combat with him.
Coming to my help, there then stepped in beside me,
    Theodora.
And then the image vanished from my inner sphere.
I once dared say to Felix and Capesius:
"It would be easy for me to bear the opposition

Now threatening my work from outside;
Even if my whole will would be shattered, –
I would be able to endure. – "
What if this image is trying to tell me
That outer opposition is but the expression
Of an inner battle – a battle with Ahriman?
Am I ready then for *this* battle as well?

Benedictus My friend, this image, as I see within your soul,
Has not yet fully ripened for you.
You can, I feel, make stronger in yourself,
The power that showed it to your spirit-eye. –
I now can sense that if you rightly strive
To bring about that strengthening,
You will create new forces, for yourself,
And also for your friends.
I feel all this;
But how it all will happen
Is hidden from my sight.

Curtain.

Scene XII

The Earth's interior. Mighty crystalline forms, broken through everywhere by streams of lava. The whole is dimly lit, partly transparent, partly translucent. Red flames towards the top appear to be compressed downwards by the roof.

Ahriman (*alone at first*)
>   Essential matter rains down from above.
>   I'll put it to my purpose.
>   Here, demonic stuff seeps
>   Into the form-realm. –
>   A human being is striving
>   To eradicate completely from himself
>   The spirit-substance that he owes to me.
>   Until this point, I could inspire him quite well;
>   But now he's much too close to that swarm of mystics
>   Who, through Benedictus's
>   Light-filled wisdom
>   Could achieve wakefulness
>   At the hour of cosmic midnight.
>   Lucifer has lost his hold on them;
>   Enabling Maria and Johannes
>   To escape his realm of light.
>   So now, with all my power,
>   I must take hold of Strader.
>   Once I have him, I'll win the others too.
>   Johannes already has hideously blunted himself
>   Upon my shadow; – he knows me well.
>   I cannot get to him – without Strader,
>   And neither to Maria.
>   And yet, perhaps, Strader will not yet be able to recognize
>   The web of tangled spirit men regard as nature
>   As my spiritual baggage –
>   And there – where I – denying all spirit
>   Am spiritually creating –
>   He will suppose

There to be nothing
But a blind, woven fabric
Of energy and matter.
The others have, I know, not ceased
To prattle on to him about my being and my realm –
But even so –
I do not think him yet completely lost.
He will quite forget that Benedictus
Sent him once half-conscious, to my realm,
To rid him of the false belief
That I am but a product of the brain
In human heads.
The only thing I'll need
If I'm to snatch him away into my realm, at the right moment,
Is a little bit of *earthly help*.
I will now summon here to me a soul
Who thinks himself so clever
That I, for him,
Am nothing more
Than a daft deception wrought by fools.
He serves me now and then, when I make use of him.

Ahriman leaves and returns with the soul of Ferdinand Reinecke. In its form, it is a kind of copy of Ahriman; when he comes in, he removes a blindfold from the person representing the soul.

His earthly intelligence
He must leave at the door.
He must not understand
What he is to *experience* here, with me.
For he's still honest;
And if he understood
Just what it is to which I will *inspire* him now,
He would wish to do nothing for me.
And later on – he must be able to forget it too.

Do you know – that *Dr. Strader* – who serves me?

The Soul of Ferdinand Reinecke
> He idly drifts about up on the earth-star.
> He tries to make his scholarly, sophisticated bunkum
>   spring to life,
> But each new puff of wind life blows just knocks it down again.
> He listens greedily to all the mystic swaggerers;
> He's half-asphyxiated already in all their mists and fog.
> And now he wants to surround Hilary in the same cloud;
> Fortunately, Hilary is kept in check by his friend, the Manager,
> For otherwise that fantasizing bunch
> Would wholly wreck his family firm
> With all their spirit-blabbering.

Ahriman
> Such prattling talk as this
> Serves me not at all.
> Right now – I just need Strader.
> As long as this one man
> Continues to believe so firmly in himself
> It will be far too easy for Benedictus
> To impart his wisdom to mankind.
> Hilary's friend might well, perhaps, help
> Lucifer; but I must strive quite differently. –
> Through Strader I must damage Benedictus.
> For if he's robbed of Strader, he will then
> Accomplish *nothing* with his other pupils.
> My adversaries, it's true, still have their power;
> For after Strader's death he will be theirs.
> However, if while he is still alive on earth,
> I can *confuse* his soul and make it lose conviction in itself,
> The result would be that Benedictus
> Could not ever again
> Place him at the forefront of his work.
> I have, you see, already read, within the Book of Destiny
> That Strader's natural days of life – will very soon be done.
> And Benedictus does not have the power to see this.

My loyal, trusty servant – you're almost too clever;
And you believe that I am but
A daft, unreal image in the minds of fools.
You're so expert in your reasoning that people listen to you.
So *go* – to Strader – very soon –
Explain to him that his machinery is wrong;
That it can never do what it has promised;
Not just because "the times are not yet favourable",
But because it has been thought out wrongly.

The Soul of Ferdinand Reinecke

For this particular task I'm well prepared.
For a long time already all my thoughts
Have only focussed on this question:
How to prove, successfully, to Strader
That he has lost his way down paths of error?
When a man has cleverly invented stuff like this,
Through many nights, at first just in his thought,
He easily believes that should it fail
The cause does not lie in the thought itself
But something from outside.
In Strader's case the situation's truly pitiful.
If he could only have kept free from all that mystic fog
And had relied but on his senses and the brilliance of his mind,
Humanity undoubtedly would have acquired
The greatest benefits from his outstanding gifts.

Ahriman   Then now – take up your weapons –
Of craft and cleverness.
Your work is to ensure
That Strader cannot ever find again
His rightful faith and confidence
In what he does and *in himself*.
When this is done, he will no longer
Wish to follow Benedictus –
Who then will be alone,

>Reliant only on himself
>And on the reasons he himself proclaims.
>But these are found *unpleasing* by mankind
>And all the more that they reveal themselves as true,
>All the more they will be hated on the earth.

The Soul of Ferdinand Reinecke
>I see already, very clearly,
>How to demonstrate to Strader
>The error in his thinking.
>His machinery is based upon an error
>Which he himself cannot become aware of.
>The dark cloud of the mystics hinders him.
>I, with all my clear and sober powers of reasoning
>Can offer him, in truth, much better service.
>I have been wanting this for many years
>But could not see the way to do it.
>Now suddenly the way lights up in me.
>I feel inspired!
>I must now go and contemplate just what I have to do
>To unmistakably convince this Strader of the truth.

Ahriman leads Reinecke's soul out of his realm and, before the person representing the soul leaves, replaces the blindfold over his eyes.

Ahriman (*alone*)
>This one can offer me, in truth, good service.
>The mystic light on earth – it burns me badly;
>I must continue working there, undisturbed,
>Without the Mystics revealing what I do.

>*Theodora's soul appears.*

Theodora's Soul
>Though you may find your way to Strader, *I*
>Am at his side; for since he found me on
>The bright-illumined paths of soul, he is

United with me – whether he must lead
His life in spirit-land or on the earth.

Ahriman   If she really does not leave him
All the while that he's on earth
Well then – my battle – will be lost.
This cannot stop me hoping, though,
That in the end he nonetheless
Might still forget her.

Curtain.

Scene XIII

A larger reception room in Hilary's house.
As the curtain opens Hilary and Romanus are in conversation together.
(Later: Capesius, Felix Balde, the Secretary; Philia.)

Hilary   With greatest pain, dear friend,
       I must confess
       That the knot of destiny
       That forms here in our circle
       Is almost crushing me.
       What can one build on
       When all around one shakes and trembles?
       Benedictus's friends, through you,
       Are kept from what we do.
       Bitter agonies of doubt
       Now weigh on Strader.
       A man who often has opposed the strivings of the mystics
       With cleverness and also – yes – with hatred –
       Has now been able to prove to him
       That he is badly wrong with his machinery –
       That this is not just blocked by outer hindrances
       But that within itself it is *impossible*.
       My life has yielded me no fruit.
       I longed for deeds
       But always lacked the thoughts
       That could have made these deeds
       Mature to ripeness.
       Barrenness of soul has caused me bitter grief.
       It was my spirit-vision alone
       Which always has sustained me.
       And yet – with Strader – even this could now deceive me.

Romanus   I've often felt as though a nightmare haunted me
       That harshly robbed my soul of any peace

When in the course of time events have shown
Your words to have been gravely wrong
And thus have made your spirit-vision
Just appear delusion.
That nightmare grew in me
Until it could become
An inner mystic teacher.
It has set free a feeling deep within me
Which now lights up my judgement. – –
You have trusted spirit-vision far too blindly;
Because of this it easily appears as error
Where it in fact was surely leading you to truth.
You have seen Strader rightly,
In spite of everything
That over-clever man has proved.

Hilary   So does your faith not waver – even now?
             Do you still keep, unshaken, the opinion
             You have had before, of Strader?

Romanus   I formed that opinion for reasons
             Which have nothing to do with Strader's friends.
             Those reasons still hold,
             Regardless of whether his machinery
             Turns out to be correct or faulty.
             Even if he was mistaken over it – so what?
             The human being has to pass through error
             To find the truth.

Hilary   You're not put off by failure? You –
             The one whose life has only ever brought *success*?

Romanus   Those people have success who have no fear of failure.
             All one has to do
             Is apply one's understanding of mysticism
             To this particular case.
             It shows quite clearly

What one has to think of Strader.
In the battle, that opens up the portals of the spirit,
He will be able to prove himself victorious;
Courageously, he will step past the Guardian
Who stands before the threshold of the spirit-world.
Within my soul I have felt deeply, through and through,
The words the strict and solemn Guardian speaks. –
I sense him now right here at Strader's side.
Whether he's able to behold him
Or but draws near to him unconsciously,
I cannot apprehend.
I believe I know Strader, though, well enough.
With his great courage, he'll attain the insight
That self-knowledge must give rise to pain.
That Will will then be his companion
Which offers itself bravely to the future,
And drawing up new strength
From powerful springs of Hope
Is able to withstand the pains of knowledge.

Hilary   My friend, I deeply thank you for these occult words.
I have so often heard them;
Yet only now, for the first time
I feel what's hidden secretly within them.
The cosmic ways are strange and hard to grasp.
I see, dear friend, that now I have to wait
Till higher powers reveal to me the way
That's in accordance with my spirit-sight.

*Hilary and Romanus leave towards the right. Capesius and Felix Balde enter
from the left. The Secretary leads them into the room.*

Secretary   I'd thought that Benedictus
Would be back today from his travels,
But he is not yet here.
If you return tomorrow

You'll be sure to meet him.

Felix Balde   Well can we speak with our friend Hilary?

Secretary   I'll go and look for him
And ask him to come over and see you.

Secretary leaves.

Felix Balde   The experience you have had is,
Without a doubt, of deep significance.
Please – could you not describe it for me once again?
It's only possible to judge these things correctly
When they are grasped, quite clearly, in the spirit.

Capesius   It was this morning, when I believed
That I was very near the Mystic Mood;
The senses – were silent; even memory – was silent.
I felt but utter openness
To what would happen in the spirit.
First there came what I well know already.
But then – the soul of *Strader*
Stood there, very clearly, before my spirit-sight.
He did not speak at first.
I had time to be aware of how awake I was.
But soon, completely clear, I heard his words as well.
"Do not leave the true Mystic Mood."
This sounded out – as if from deep within him.
Then he said – emphasizing strongly every word:
"To strive for nothing; only to be still and at peace;
The inner being of the soul wide open – ;
That is the Mystic Mood. It awakens
Of itself – quite unsought for in life's stream –
When the human soul does rightly grow in strength,
When, empowered in thinking, it rightly seeks the spirit.
The mood may well descend in quiet hours,
But also 'midst the storm of action; it then

Wants only that the soul
Does not, in thoughtlessness,
Evade the fragile, tender vision
Of what is happening in spirit."

Felix Balde This almost sounds just like an echo
Of my words – though not exactly as I meant them.

Capesius When one thinks about it carefully
One can also find it means
The opposite of your words. –
This is even more the case
When one considers
What he then went on to say.
"If someone, though, awakens artificially
The Mystic Mood,
They lead their inner being
Only into *themselves.*
Indeed, over the realm of light
They weave a web of darkness,
The darkness of what works in their own souls.
Whoever seeks for this, through Mysticism,
Destroys their spirit-sight
With mystical delusion."

Felix Balde This can be nothing else than my own words,
Reversed and twisted by the character of Strader,
Resounding then in you as an appalling Mystic Error.

Capesius Then Strader, in the end, spoke these words too:
"Human beings cannot find the spirit world
If they attempt to enter it by seeking.
Within that soul who over many years
Seeks for a *mood* – and nothing else –
The truth cannot resound."

Philia appears, who can only be seen by Capesius. Felix Balde reveals by his attitude that he does not understand the words that follow.

Philia   Capesius, if you pay heed
To what now shows itself to you, unsought,
Within your seeking,
You soon will be empowered
By all that weaves within the many-coloured light;
In living images, like very beings,
It wholly will pervade you now,
Because it is revealed to you by forces of your soul.
What shines from your own Self's most Sunlit being
Will be dimmed down by Saturn's ripened wisdom.
Then to your vision there will be unveiled
What you, as earthly human being, can understand.
And I will guide you then, myself,
To that great Guardian who keeps watch
Upon the mighty threshold of the spirit.

Felix Balde   Words resound from spheres I do not know
But as their tones create no light-filled life
They are not full reality for me.

Capesius   The counsel Philia gives will be my guide
So that in future
There will also be revealed to me in spirit
What is already understandable to me
Within my sphere of life on earth.

Curtain.

Scene XIV

The same room as in the previous scene. When the scene begins, Hilary's wife in conversation with the Manager of the firm.

Hilary's Wife

>It almost seems the deed
>My husband still considers so essential
>Is not desired by destiny itself –
>When one considers
>Just how tangled are the threads
>That power has spun into the *knot of life*
>That binds us here so tightly.

Manager   A woven knot of destiny,
>Which, to human minds,
>Can certainly appear
>Impossible to solve or to undo. – –
>------------
>Well, then – it must be cut!
>------------
>I see no other possibility
>Than that there has to be *a cut*
>Between your husband
>And my whole sphere of life. – –

Hilary's Wife

>To separate from you. – No –
>That is something my husband could never do.
>For it would contradict in every way
>The spirit of the firm,
>Which has been handed down by his dear father
>And which his son continues to be loyal to.

Manager   Has this loyalty
>Not long ago already
>Been betrayed?

The goals that Hilary is seeking now
Live in a wholly opposite direction
From the one that spirit
Always wished to go in.

Hilary's Wife

All my husband's happiness in life
Now hinges on the realisation of this goal.
Since, like a lightning-flash of thought,
It sprang to life within him,
I have seen how he has utterly transformed. –
Life, before, had only brought about in him
A bleak and desperate barrenness of soul,
Which he kept carefully hidden
Even from his closest friends,
And which thus all the more
Would eat away at him within.
He felt himself to be quite insignificant,
For no thoughts ever sprouted in his soul
Which could have seemed to him *worthy* of life.
When then the plan rose up before him –
The project – of bringing mystic life
Into activity – he was made young again –
He was a different man – and always happy.
With this goal he felt himself for the first time *worthy of life.* –
That you could have stood against him –
He couldn't have imagined – until he saw it.
And when he did – it struck him harder
Than almost any blow
That life has ever dealt him.
If you knew how much he suffers because of you
I am sure that you would soften the harshness of your stance.

Manager

If I were to go against my own conviction
It would seem to me that I had lost
All human dignity.

It will be very difficult
To see myself
With Strader working next to me;
But I have decided to take on this burden
Because Romanus supports it,
Who I understand,
Now that he's spoken to me about Strader.
What he said to me
I know to be the beginning of my own spirit-schooling.
From his words flamed forth a power
Which passed across immediately into my soul;
Never in my life had I experienced
Such inner power as this.
The advice he gives must be of great importance to me
Even if, as yet, I cannot fully follow it with understanding.
Romanus only gives support to Strader;
The contributions of the other Mystics, in his eyes,
Would not just be a hindrance to the work,
But would, he holds, be even *dangerous* for themselves.
I value Romanus's opinion *so highly*
That I must now believe that if Strader
Cannot find his way to act without his friends,
Then this would have to be for him a sign of destiny.
It would clearly show to him
He should, for now, remain beside his friends
And only later bring about
From his interior mystic striving
Impulses for actual deeds in outer life.
The fact that he has been standing in these recent days
Much closer to these friends than ever before,
After they had been more distant for a while,
Leads me to believe that this indeed
Will be his situation,
Even if it means, for now,
He'll have to see his goals as wholly lost.

Hilary's Wife
>You look at Strader only through those eyes
>That have been opened for you by Romanus.
>Try and see him quite impartially.
>He can so wholly give himself to spirit-life
>That he appears transported from the realm of earth.
>He stands completely in the presence of the spirit –
>And in the living presence of Theodora.
>When one speaks with him, it's just as if
>She too were there before one.
>Many are the mystics
>Quite well able to imprint
>The spirit-message into words,
>So that, when they are thought about,
>They bring conviction.
>What Strader speaks
>Works within his very speech itself.
>One sees he very little values
>Experience of the spirit which is merely inward,
>And knows itself quite satisfied within the realm of feeling –
>That as a mystic
>He will place before all else
>The impulse for research.
>And therefore he does not confuse, through mysticism,
>The sense for science,
>Which shows itself so practically
>Of such great service in our lives. –
>Please try and see this in him –
>And through him understand as well
>That one will have to value far more highly
>*His own* judgement of his friends
>Than the one arrived at by Romanus.

Manager   In this situation,
>So far from my accustomed sphere of thought,

Romanus' judgement is for me
The solid ground
Upon which I can stand. –
If I must go into a realm
Which brings me very near to mysticism,
Then I will absolutely need such guidance
Someone can only give me who has won my trust
Through that within them
I can fully understand.

> *The Secretary enters.*

You walk in all distraught, my friend. What's happened?

Secretary (*hesitant*)
Dr Strader... died... a few hours ago.

Manager   He's died. Strader?

Hilary's Wife
Strader – dead – Where's Hilary?

Secretary   He's in his room...
As if paralysed by the news
Just brought to him from Strader's house.

> *Hilary's wife leaves. The Secretary follows her.*

Manager (*alone*)
He's died. Strader! Is this reality?

Is that deep spirit-sleep
Of which I've heard so much
Already touching me?
A serious, sombre face is shown
By that great power of destiny
Who here is pulling on the threads.
O, my little soul,
What power so seized your thread of destiny

Within his hand
That now it's inter-woven in this knot.

Whatever must happen, will happen!

Why have these words never left me
Since the moment Strader spoke them
In front of Hilary and myself?
They sounded out
As if they'd come to him
From quite another world; –
Spoken by one as if transported
Into spirit-realms! –
O what then is it that should happen? –
I feel indeed that in that moment
In those very words
I was seized hold of by the spirit-world –
Its language sounds out to me – ;
Sounds out in serious tones; –
How may I learn to understand it?

Curtain.

Scene XV

The same room as in the previous scene. The nurse of Dr. Strader is sitting there,
waiting. After the curtain opens, the Secretary enters the room; (later Benedictus.
Ahriman.)

Secretary   Benedictus will soon be here
             To receive your message from you himself. –
             He's been away, but has just returned.
             What a great, extraordinary man was Dr. Strader!
             I didn't really have faith, you know, at the beginning,
             In Hilary's colossal, far-reaching project;
             But as I was often present, when Strader
             Showed him what was necessary for the work,
             All of my objections swiftly fell away.
             He was always so alert in spirit, so intelligent,
             And had the strongest sense
             For what was possible
             And what was fitting to the purpose.
             And yet, he always strove as well
             To find the final goal
             Solely from the matter in hand –
             As it revealed itself –
             And to presuppose nothing, in thought,
             Beforehand.
             The man behaved exactly as a mystic should –
             Like somebody who climbs a mountain peak
             Because they wish to see the heavenly view.
             They wait till they have reached the top – and do
             Not first think up some image of it in their minds.

Nurse   In the busy, active stream of life
             You have known a man
             With mighty gifts and noble strength of spirit;
             In the brief while

When I could carry out for him
His last services on earth
I have been able to marvel
At his lofty soul. This dear soul
Which, apart from seven years of rare happiness,
Always walked through earthly life alone.
The Mystics offered him their wisdom.
He, though, needed Love.
His great desire for deeds –
This was also love –
For love, in order to reveal itself
Will show itself in many different forms.
All that this soul sought for, in his spirit-striving,
Was just as needed by the noble fire
That burned within his being
As the healing balm of restful sleep
Is needed by the body
After many hours of arduous, creative work.

Secretary   And the source of all his creative work
Was in the mystic wisdom;
Every single thing he did was always filled by this,
And in the most beautiful of ways.

Nurse   Because by his very nature
He always had to love
And to unite his soul completely
With all that wished to make itself
The mission of his life.
Even the very final thoughts he had were for the work
To which he'd given himself – with so much love. – –
Just the way that other people part from those they love
So the soul of Strader
Left behind the earthly work
Into which he selflessly had poured his love.

Secretary   He lived, within the kernel of his being, in spirit,
             And Theodora always stood before his gaze
             Just like a living soul – ; that is the way true mystics feel.

Nurse   Yes. For solitude had joined them both together.
             Even in death she stood before him. –
             It seemed to him
             That she was calling him away
             To spirit-worlds
             For the completion of his work.
             A few hours before he died
             He wrote these words for Benedictus
             That now I will deliver to the Mystics' guide and teacher.

             And thus must life go on
             In these our present days on earth,
             Mysterious and full of riddles; –
             Illumined, though, by Sun-like beings, like Strader,
             From whom, revolving round like planets,
             The others all receive the Light
             That wakens them and brings new life to birth.

                  Benedictus enters; the Secretary leaves.

             Before he grew too weak
             Strader managed still
             To write these few last lines.
             I now deliver them to you, the Mystics' friend.

Benedictus   And once he'd written down these words,
             Where then was he, in his soul, until the end?

Nurse   At first his final plans in life
             Were living in his thoughts. Theodora then
             Was wholly there for him in spirit.
             Feeling this, his soul did delicately free itself
             And left his body's covering behind.

Benedictus You loyal, faithful being
I deeply thank you for the service
You were able to perform for him on earth.

The Nurse leaves. Benedictus reads Strader's final words.

"My friend, (dear Benedictus),
When I felt myself almost completely shattered,
Recognizing that the opposition to my own creations
Was not caused merely from outside,
But that inner failings in the fundamental thought itself
Were hindering the further progress of the work,
I saw that image once again
Which I described to you
A little while ago.
This time, though, the image ended in a different way.
It was not Ahriman, this time,
Who fought against me in the battle;
A messenger from spirit-realms appeared beside him,
Whose very form, I clearly felt,
Was that of *my own thought,*
So badly filled with error.
And then I had to make myself remember
Your words about the need for strengthening
The power of the forces of my soul.
And as I did so, then that messenger from spirit-realms
Immediately disappeared. – "

There follow after this a few more words –
I cannot read them, though – a chaos
Weaving a veil of cloudéd thought –
Hides them from me.

Ahriman appears; Benedictus sees him.

Who are you, who appears within my soul's horizon –
Emerging like a shadow from my chaos?

Ahriman (*to himself*)
        He sees me very well, but does not know yet who I am.
        And so he will not bring to me that agonizing pain
        If I attempt to work now at his side.

          To Benedictus.

        I can give your further news about what Strader now
        Is wishing to confide in you –
        Both for the help and service it may be to you –
        And for your pupils' onward mystic path.

Benedictus The mystic group around me
        Will always know itself united
        With the soul of Strader,
        Although there is no further bridge to him
        In sense-existence.
        But if a messenger from spirit-worlds is wishing to approach us,
        And to bring revelations from the realms where Strader
            now abides,
        Then he has first of all to *win* our confidence.
        This he can only do
        If he appears in such a way
        Before our spirit-sight
        That he may be *completely known.*

Ahriman   But you are only striving for *self-knowledge*;
        So if a spirit-being, different from you,
        That wants to prove itself of service,
        Can only be permitted by your side if able to be *known*,
        It first of all will need to show itself to you
        As part of *your own self.*

Benedictus Whoever you may be, you only serve the Good,
        If you do not desire to strive within yourself, alone,
        But willingly, will lose yourself in human thinking,
        And through this rise, renewed, within the world's evolving.

Ahriman   So now it's time for me to leave
            His spirit-sphere
            As fast as possible;
            For from the moment that his spirit-sight
            Can also *think* me, as in truth I am,
            There will create itself, quite soon, within his thinking,
            A portion of that power, which will, eventually, annihilate me.

            Ahriman disappears.

Benedictus Only now do I recognize him – Ahriman –
            Who flees from here, himself,
            And yet creates within me
            Knowledge of his being, in thought.
            He strives forever to confuse all human thinking
            For through an error handed down from ancient days
            He wants to see in it the source of all his sufferings.
            He does not know as yet
            Redemption will be only his in future,
            When, in the mirror of this thinking,
            He can then refind himself anew.
            And so, although he shows himself indeed to human beings,
            He does not do so as in truth he feels himself to be.
            And thus, with Strader,
            He revealed himself – and yet concealed himself as well,
            And sought to make that moment,
            With the opportunities it brings,
            Serve his own advantage.
            He hoped, through this
            To damage Strader's friends as well;
            But in the future
            He will not be able to disguise his being
            From my spirit-pupils;
            Whenever he is holding sway within their inner world
                and vision,

They then should find the power, in wakefulness,
    to think him too. –
My pupils now
Should rightly recognize and understand
The many different forms he takes,
All seeking to conceal him from us,
When he has to reveal himself to human souls.

But you, O soul of Strader,
Ripened in the power of the Sun,
Who has, through strengthening the forces of your soul,
Compelled the messenger of Error to disappear,
You will shine upon your friends –
And be for them
A radiant spirit-star;
Your light in future
Always will irradiate
The being of Maria and of Johannes;
They'll find their way, therefore, through you,
To arm themselves, with ever greater strength,
For all their spirit-tasks in future –
And they will prove themselves
Revealers of the light within the soul,
Through mighty, inner strength of thought,
Even then
When over bright and fully-wakened spirit-vision,
Grey, bleak Ahriman, dulling down wisdom,
Attempts to spread the darkening night of chaos.

Curtain.

Wynstones Press
publishes and distributes a range of
Books, Advent Calendars, Cards and Prints.
For further information please see:

www.wynstonespress.com
info@wynstonespress.com